SO YOU WANT TO BE
A STRIPPER?
2ND EDITION

GO TO OUR WEBSITE FOR THESE TITLES

http://www.djehutiwritingandpublishing.com/

Available Now

FUTURE PRINTS

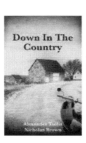 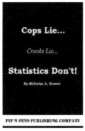  

 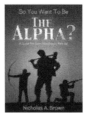

Coming Soon

ALSO IN THE FUTURE

- *So You Want To Get Your Life Right?*
- *So You Want To Be The Boss Lady?*
- *Another Day, Another Death* (Graphic Novel)
- *So You Want To Be A Cheapskate?*
- *Next: Welcome to the Party Line* (Suspense/Thriller)
- *Gossip from the Children of Nightingale*
- *So You Want To Visit Miami?*
- *8 to 12 Times: When Black Towns or Neighborhoods Broke Bread*
- *The Business Secrets of Marcus Garvey and Other Black Leaders*

So You Want to Be a Stripper?

Comprehensive Guide on Going from Girl-Next-Door to Pole Dancing Diva

2ND Edition

Written by Nicholas Brown & Elsa Joseph

Book Cover Art: Sandra Jean-Pierre

To the exotic dancer game, for all the good times,

bad experiences, and ugly turn of events,

thank you for I'm still standing.

TABLE OF CONTENTS

CHAPTER 1:
INTROS, WARNINGS
& REASONS

Thank you for investing in my words. In my life, learning to be up front and raw about things is always the best policy. You can lie and front all you want, but after reading this if you still choose to dance for your money, then it's on you. I'm giving advice I wished was given to me before stepping onto a stage. People do what they will, so don't blame me for helping somebody's little girl get in then out this game.

I've been at this for years, mostly in Miami. I've danced at the high-end clubs, in the ghetto spots, and hole-in-the-walls where space was very limited. I've seen things, been around people I thought I'd never meet, and befriended those in society who are role models. This hustle has opened my eyes, showing how low some men will go while being wild and free, and how far certain women will stoop for an extra dollar. It's because of what transpired with me, you will avoid unnecessary traps.

To the normal women going to school, working those 8, 12, and even 16 hour shifts, much of what I divulge in this book you can use in everyday life. You will learn a few things about setting yourself apart from others when in a competitive job environment. And yes, please believe that I know some moves that'll have your man appreciate what you do for him.

Remember, those who decided on their own freewill to shake what they got could've jumped into the daily grind, but chose this route. So after reading, don't cry if you get caught up because you ignored what I suggested. I wrote this out of love and in the hopes that curious women find their way into something else. In time your cute little body ain't going to last. Slimmer girls, with tighter bodies, and younger faces turn 18 every day, so how will you keep up after a while? There are exceptions to the rule but do you want to take that risk?

Games are meant to be played, so knowing when to quit while you're ahead is your best bet. In time, you'll see what can make or break you but I want to see you at the winners circle -- gaining a world of knowledge without losing your mind, body or soul. Why I started may differ from why you're starting. With every major choice in a person's life there are always reasons, so I'll get into what I've come across in this portion of the manual.

Before age 18, some girls I encountered were either:

- Rebellious kids who did what they wanted
- Teenage runaways or teenage mothers
- Sexually abused and felt like their physical beauty is what made them pretty or special
- Met a pimp who put her under his guidance
- Came from negative and dysfunctional family environments with drug abuse or alcoholism
- Had weak father figures or no father figures at all.

Other girls without the harsh backgrounds, when they were teens, probably thought being a sexy exotic dancer was glamorous and empowering. Some had an older cousin or friend they looked up to who danced, seeing how well they got paid and dressed; and in certain situations, the two family members or friends started working at the club together at the same time.

I've met girl who were intrigued through rap music videos as kids, or overheard uncles and older male cousins talking about the strip club. While some were sick of being broke, and didn't want an entry level job, working for low pay. Others simply thought they had what it took to be a dancer then went for it once they turned 18, 19 or 20.

Women between ages 21 - 28 who started dancing were either:

- Out on their own with bills piling up
- In college or a technical school and they couldn't pay tuition

- Worked a normal job but something major occurred. Examples: pregnancy, their man getting locked up, or an immediate family member took sick
- Like with the younger girls, a pimp guided them in
- Have a criminal record and found it hard getting a job
- A friend suggested they try it along with them
- A small few actually dreamed about being a dancer when they were younger.

All in all, it boils down to money in the end. How each person spends their cash is their business. But what's needed to survive shall always cloud our best judgments, especially when you don't have a pot to piss in or a window to throw it out of.

FAIR WARNING: Sins of the Life

Fast money is don't last money is a motto you better keep in mind. You're heading into a game where much of the seven deadly sins can show up on a weekly basis. You will get to know the pride of diva dancers, and witness the avarice of the hustlers spending the big money. You will be approached by lust filled -- sex craved customers. The envy from whorish and slothful dancers, sleeping around for small amounts of cash, will be heard in their snide remarks. Prepare for the rumors about the gluttonous club owners standing to make thousands of dollars off your labor. And beware the wrath of jealous lovers or rivals beefing over who knows what.

4

You're going to meet people with shared interests and even view them as family, but thoroughly study those around you because in the beginning there are no friends. Everybody isn't your enemy, but remain vigilant because people will try screwing you over emotionally, sexually and/or financially. A pretty girl is seen as meek by most people, so be smart about every step you take.

You're entering a field where nakedness or partial nudity is a key requirement. Customers will touch you in ways, or say things you truly don't want to hear. Some nights will be so slow that you end up owing money to the club; and new girls or seasoned dancers will try to out best you, if you can't entice the customers.

You're stepping into a world where weak minds either end up on drugs, become alcoholics, abused or pimped by certain kinds of customers, or just plain lose their minds or faith in humanity. Some people may know of your life as a dancer and automatically stereotype you in the worst ways. The moral and/or religious folks may judge you, knowing they don't have any right doing so, but need someone to insult for them to feel better about their backsliding. Family and close friends may judge you harshly as well because they feel you can do better.

You're going to be asked "why are you here", or told "you're too pretty to be in this club." Your parents, if they care, may be disappointed or even angered by your choice, feeling they

5

let you down somehow. If you have a kid or kids, people may assume you're an unfit parent, and feel they must keep tabs on you and your kid(s). Regardless of the fact you get topless or naked for money, you're still a woman who deserves respect, who's having a tough time for now. But these are but a few things you must keep in mind. I'm not trying to scare you straight, you're grown do what you want, but know that I did this because I care.

The names of clubs in Miami have changed -- the names and faces that frequented these spots have come and gone. Nothing stays the same except how this game is played. For example, two clubs that exist as of now (November 2015) in Miami are Tootsie's and King of Diamonds. Tootsie's was a normal sized club in a small shopping plaza -- now it's in what was a large warehouse. King of Diamonds (the legendary KOD) was first Crazy Horse, until it was sold to new owners.

The main point I'm making about the backgrounds of these clubs is the fact that you aren't doing anything new. So if you think you're coming to change the game, be larger than life –- many tried but so few break into bigger and better things. This is a stepping stone and not a lifestyle, don't ever forget that.

Once again I ask:

"So you want to be a stripper?"

CHAPTER 2:

NOTHING TO IT BUT TO DO IT

After contemplating whether you want to dance or not, the next step is figuring which club you fit into. Scout the more popular clubs first, seeing for your self the environment, and asking the dancers some questions. You must find out if a place is safe and has standards.

Most classy clubs tend to look for what's called the baby doll or Barbie look, which can either be petite and sexy or tall and slim like a fashion model. Thickness (nice round butt, top heavy or both) is cool, but it must be tone, with little to no belly fat. Most good looking girls with thickness tend to dance at popular urban clubs.

Some clubs allow plus sized dancers, or women with body deformities such as scars or stretch marks. But do know clubs that accept most body shapes and types, their level of quality, safety and customers goes down. You'll be dancing at your own risk by doing so. Keep in mind, if the club doesn't make you feel safe then don't dance there. You can make money in all clubs, but in the well-to-do places, you're nearly guaranteed to make good money.

What you're looking for when it comes to a decent club:

- Security that must wear a dress shirt, tie and jacket/blazer
- The club has a valid liquor license
- Large topless clubs because fully nude spots can be shady
- If customers must follow a dress code
- Management that actually care for dancers' safety
- Police aren't always there for violent crimes or lewd acts
- Nationally or internationally recognized celebrities and shot callers are always in there

I implore that you workout and eat right ahead of time. Regardless of how fabulous you are as a person, this is a business geared toward the fantasies of men. Most men of means like seeing slim, fit & tone, or fit & tone thick women (hour glass figures or pear shaped women), so please put your ego to the side and get your body right. The more appealing you are the more money you can make at the right clubs. Plus you must remember, pole dancing classes are work outs, so if you aren't in shape for the pole, you won't look good and can even get hurt on stage.

Unless they're having an open audition for girls at a club, go to the club by yourself where you know your body type is accepted. Auditions can be fierce because the competition may be veteran dancers who already have the skills. Always go in the daytime, and when you do, ask an employee of the club for the day shift or day manager. Someone who has say in hiring a girl will come out to see how you look. If they like what they see, they'll give you either a basic application, Independent Contractor form, or a Sub-Contractor form to fill out. They'll also ask for a picture I.D., and what your dancer name will be on your application.

Quick Advice: When picking a dancer name, try choosing one that will leave customers wondering who you are after hearing it. The right name will set you apart from the competition quickly.

All clubs have age restrictions. They usually look for women between 18 and 30 years of age, and you must be at least 21 to have an alcoholic drink. You may get hired by some clubs if you're above age of 30, but only if you still look young and vibrant. If you're under age 18, and use false identification to get hired, you're risking not only getting yourself in trouble, but also the club's owner. Don't get someone else in trouble for your deception.

After turning your application and other information, most clubs will ask you to return for a tryout, if a club doesn't hire or audition you on the spot. They usually tell you, but just in case, ask them what to wear and what not to wear for your audition. Based on your state's laws on what's acceptable will dictate your outfit, and even if you'll keep your job or not. I suggest you get lingerie or a cheap $10 - $20 costume from an adult novelty store, and high heels between three to six inches (7.62 cm to 15.24 cm) high.

When you return, it's best to have what we call a *dance bag*. The bag should contain a change of clothes, shoes, deodorant, body spray, lotion, hair brush, feminine wipes and other supplies. And please, have music ready (two – four songs) for your tryout as well.

Quick Advice: For your audition, have some sexy moves that you've practiced ahead of time. Make sure you do your moves in the heels you'll audition in. Many clubs have an amateur night, with some offering cash prizes to the winners. These are great ways to try your moves and kill some of those butterflies in your stomach. And if you haven't taken a class, or practiced ahead of time elsewhere then don't get on the pole.

The managers and other trusted employees will help evaluate whether you have what it takes. If the audition goes well, the manager should tell you the rules and regulations of the club, which are often posted in the dressing room in case you need reminding.

RULES, REGULATIONS & LEARNING THE ROPES

Along with the rules, the manager will tell you about the club's house fee (also called "tip out" in certain clubs) dancers must pay. The house fee covers payment to the DJ, security guards/bouncers, and sometimes the bartenders or bar backs. Depending upon the club, it's paid either before you start your shift or at the end of your shift. Based on what shift you work, the fee can be from $30.00 to $100.00.

Different clubs have a system in how they choose which girls go on which shifts. Some clubs put girls on the day shift (from noon to around eight p.m.), during the work week then when ready, put them on night shift (eight p.m. until closing). Other clubs, if they're wowed by a girl's moves and beauty, she may start at night shift right away, but during the week. Once a girl has an understanding of what is needed from her, and has the right energy and presence, she'll work nights during the weekends, where the crowds are usually larger.

Quick Advice: Some owners own more than one gentleman's club, so find out which ones. You may get recruited to fill in space for these other places, and they may not be as classy as the one you wanted to dance at. The girls can be meaner, customers may be crazy and/or broke, or security and management may be uncaring. So really do some digging, and ask a ton of questions on where you will be dancing. Once again, if you don't like the spot they're trying to send you, then go some where else.

Slow days for both shifts are Monday, Tuesday and Wednesday. Fast days and nights are Thursdays thru Sunday, unless there's a special event on a slow night. On fast days, during the day time, the flow of money usually doesn't pick up until after four or five p.m. Different clubs have different tempos, so it's best to ask which days are fast or slow.

New dancers get placed on a schedule or are told verbally when their schedules are. If you don't come on your scheduled times, the club might fine you. This fine can range between $25 – $30 dollars, and higher depending on the club. As I stated earlier there are house rules you must keep in mind.

The ones to memorize are:

- No fighting with customers, dancers or other employees of the club
- Never show up high or drunk
- Don't have sex in the champagne room or V.I.P sections
- Don't sleep or have any sexual relationships with managers, staff, or customers period.

Breaking any of these rules can get you fired, or worse, locked up behind bars. And if you're having relations with management, please understand that he most likely is sleeping with another dancer in the club, or has a significant other already. So don't get mad if you see him being overly friendly with a fellow dancer, or his woman. Remember always, that you're there to get your money, and not treat the club as a dating service.

Before stepping into the club, bouncers will check your bags for any weapons or alcohol you purchased outside the club. Some girls may try to sneak things in for their boyfriends or a customer their dating. Unless they're in law enforcement, if you're dating someone that must carry a weapon that badly, I suggest you leave them alone. You're working to make your way into a better life -- not look rich and die trying.

The dress code for dancers is fairly simple. You'll probably start with lingerie and bathing suits, then later as your money and customer base grows, get more elaborate costumes. I'll explain how to style these up, along with your makeup and looks later in the manual. For now just know every outfit plays a role depending on if the club is full nudity, or only a topless bar.

Quick Advice: Every three to six months, at random, a club's owner, management and staff are called in for a mandatory club meeting. These meetings are used to reiterate current rules, announce new rules & codes they'll be implementing, and upcoming events. They even ask people, especially the dancers, to talk about what problems they have with another person in the club. Girls can get catty, but at least folks will voice their grievances. At times, even though they're supposed to say what's bothering them about others at the meetings, some girls still want to fight. So remain as diplomatic as possible when at the club. If being diplomatic isn't working then see about going to a different club. It's always best to leave with a good reputation, especially if you're making money. No one wants to work with a person who has a bad attitude.

More Quick Advice: If you miss a mandatory club meeting, a club may fine you -- depending on the club, $50.00 - $100.00.

Some clubs assign you a locker with your name placed above it on tape, or alphabet stickers that spell your name like on a NFL team during preseason. Other clubs offer lockers on a first come, first service bases every day. If this is so, at the end of your shift clean out the locker or else management might cut your lock and toss your stuff.

Be smart and try not to have money in your locker, or place anything of value in there. When in the dressing rooms, keep your stuff away from others the best you can. Some women know how to pick locks. Other thieves may see that you made money and they didn't, so they'll lie to management saying you have an item of theirs in your locker. All while you're on the dance floor, they'll tell management you said it was okay to break the lock because you didn't want to find the key. They'll come up with whatever lie sounds best in order to rob you.

THREE CATAGORIES OF GIRLS

It takes a multi-talented dancer who can work all three facets, but after sometime the category of girl you fall under are *floor hustlers*, *stage girl*, or *V.I.P Pro*. Each girl gets paid, but each has a different skill set others may not be equipped with.

All categories have personalities I'll further explain later, but if you can master each, you'll minimize the chances of having a low paying night. A low paying night is always a bad night, so stay in your lane.

Floor Dancers or Floor Hustlers

Floor hustlers as the name implies work the floor. They go from table to table, guy to guy seeing who wants a dance. Floor hustlers are usually great conversationalist, who can charm most men. Great floor hustlers can read a room to see whose buying single drinks, from whose buying bottles and at what time of day. A good floor dancer can figure out who's spending big, from those catching drink specials before eight p.m. If your gift of gab isn't there, or you feel that being a floor hustler is too much work, then don't try it.

Stage Girls

Stage girls are the ladies on the pole putting on acrobatic displays, or partnering up with other girls on busy nights for freak shows or stage performances. Some of these girls can floor hustle, but many have poor people skills. They expect guys to be amazed by what they did on stage to pull tips, or have guys requesting them for dances. The only downside is that half the crowd may not have seen them dance, or paid any attention to them while they were on stage. It's best to have some floor skills if you're taking this route.

A special group of stage girls are the *feature dancers* or the *headline performer*. These are the ones who built a name with their performances, business sense, networking and promotional skills. They bring in crowds because their stage routines, personalities, professionalism, and physical beauty are so topnotch, they leave club patrons in awe. Feature dancers are like mercenaries because they only go to the clubs paying what they demand, and promote their arrivals properly.

Club owners pay these women to dance at their club, even if they have to fly them out. Headline performers are stars of the dancer circuits. They sometimes are in music videos with a few who were in adult magazines and/or porn flicks. The more interesting personalities made it onto reality television shows and even had roles in movies.

From my understanding, clubs pay feature dancers an upfront fee before coming to the club, and keep all tips they get from customers. The performers who are nationally or internationally known, with business sense, may get part or all of the money coming from the door (the door is what patrons pay to get in the club), as well as tips and an upfront fee.

For example: an owner might bring in a known headline performer by paying them $20,000 upfront, plus whatever tips are thrown onstage for that dancer.

V.I.P Pros or V.I.P girls

V.I.P Pros or *V.I.P girls* are dancers who are hardly on the floor. You'll see them on stage dancing once or twice, but they would rather get a customer into the V.I.P or champagne rooms to work their magic.

Be warned though, not all but a good amount of the dancers in this category are known for doing sexual favors for extra money. If you aren't like that, then avoid any advice from these girls, unless it's on how to please your own significant other. You never know if the guy you're trying these tricks on will slap handcuffs on you, taking you in for soliciting.

Quick Advice: Never get money for VIP dances afterward. You get that money upfront before you do anything.

More Quick Advice: If you ever feel lost during your first few weeks, ask a female bartender or server any dancer related questions. It's a strong chance that they were dancers as well. Some girls may see you as competition and get very bitchy. So have the more respected and honest female staff, who were ex-dancers guide you.

When it comes to your musical selections, some DJs will play songs you prepared on a CD or flash drive before your shift. If you can, make sure you get songs that wake you up and get you moving. Some of the lower quality clubs don't have DJs, they have juke boxes. In the latter situation, if possible, have three songs in mind you enjoy dancing to.

Under normal circumstances, when it comes to musical selections "DJ's Choice" is in effect. This means whatever music is chosen, the DJ does so based on what the DJ feels is appropriate for the crowd. Even if you beg, if a DJ says "DJs Choice" don't bother asking again. Managers are supposed to explain this to you (or at least veteran dancers) about what to do when unclothing yourself while dancing onstage.

The unclothing onstage process goes like this:
- Remain fully dressed during your first song. You're mostly teasing, doing some light pole work, and getting comfortable being up there.
- For the second song, depending upon the club being topless or fully nude, you take off your top or bottom.
- If the club is an all nude establishment, by the third song, you get all the way in the buff.

The minimum amount of songs to dance to when on stage is three, with six being the maximum. But if you're doing more than four songs, you're usually on stage with another dancer, referred to as a stage partner. Also if you dance more than four songs, if the DJ notices that the crowd is into your performance, he'll be sure to put on the best tracks that'll bring the party to life.

When on stage and there's a busy crowd, some girls who work great as a pair, will do what's called a *Freak Show*. These shows are done at random when the club is packed, drinks are flowing, guys are tipping, and money is circulating. They're a great way to keep the party's momentum going.

Freak Shows are decided by the dancers, so it's best you and your stage partner have a routine practiced, along with props you will want to use. With the props, they can range from sex toys to alcoholic beverage bottles, and depending on the club, even snakes or hot candle wax. If it's not illegal and keeps all eyes on you plus customers happy, then do it. For when done right, the tips thrown on stage from a Freak Show can payout nicely -- serious stage dancers can always do superb Freak Shows.

When it comes to tips being thrown, depending on the club, they'll allow dancers to walk around and ask for tips, after being on stage. Some guys who like how you look or danced while on stage, or both, will ask for a dance from you. So be on the lookout for those who tipped you or paid you extra attention while on stage. Once off stage, if you charm that customer right, he may spend all his cash on you.

When asking for tips, be courteous. It's good to approach customers saying, "Hi, how are you, would you like to tip me for my stage performance?" Be sure to have a winning smile when doing so. Don't be blunt when asking for a tip by saying, "can I get a tip?" It comes off as rude, demanding and without tact.

Quick Advice: If you can, don't try procuring dances from customers nearest to the stage, or what some clubs call the tip rail area, if a another dancer is on stage. Avoid problems by not possibly agitating another dancer because you took tip money from her. Only talk to customers in the tip rail area when the club is packed, and there are more than enough customers the girl on stage can't get to.

Last but not least, the kinds of dances you perform for the customers, and how much to charge for dances. The first dance customers may request is the *table top*. A table top dance is when you're dancing sexy in front of a customer, but little to no physical contact is made. Certain clubs such as the hood or lower end spots tend to let physical contact pass.

Grabbing a dancer's rear end, breasts, or even slipping a finger into a dancer's vaginal area may slide in lower class places. In most lower end spots, a table top costs $5.00 per song or two -- and can be as much as $15.00 per song or two at upscale clubs.

The next dance you will be asked to do is a *lap dance*, or what some places call a *friction dance* or *full friction*. A lap dance is when a dancer is grinding on a customer's lap and/or crotch region. While doing this, you must wear some kind of bottom piece, be it boy shorts, g-string or bikini bottom.

No touching is to occur, but as stated with table tops, hood or lower end clubs may let it go without penalty. In most hood or lower class places, a lap dance is $10.00 per song or two, while at classier joints its $20.00 or $25.00 per song or two.

Quick Advice: In certain clubs, dancers aren't allowed to touch customers. Depending on the club, you can be fined for breaking the "do not touch rule."

<u>MARK THESE WORDS</u>

One of the stigmas of an exotic dancer is being perceived as escorts or prostitutes. I admit many girls do find themselves turning tricks. Nearly every new dancer goes in just dancing for money. But some girls have a run of bad luck, or unexpected events so overwhelming that they'll accept what a patron or two or more constantly offered to pay them for an hour or less of sexual favors.

Unless you want to live with that feeling of disgust, don't do it. With some women they easily slip into that side of the game, and find it hard to get out. Your body can hold up but for so long until it's warn out. So please, even if you must get a second job, avoid that route at all costs. Closed legs don't get fed, and a closed mouth may keep you out a house, but HIV, AIDS, Herpes, and other things to come aren't curable yet and last forever.

CHAPTER 3:

WHO YOU MAY MEET

In chapter two, I stated the categories of the dancers. In this portion you will be introduced the arch types of not only the girls, but the customers and staff as well. Smiling faces, two-faced, and screwed faces giving the stink eye can be found among these people, so keep alert at all times.

<u>Owners, Management & Staff</u>

The owners calls shots, chooses management, hires talent scouts and in few cases picks the girls. You may see or meet them, but in most cases they'll be something like a ghost. Do your best making the owners pleased to have you around.

Managers, bartenders, cooks & kitchen workers, servers/waitresses, and security (bouncers) work in shifts. You usually have one manager working in the day, from noon until eight p.m. One or two managers work at night from eight p.m. until close, depending upon whether it's the weekend or not. There are, based on the size and class level of club, between three – eight managers in total. During a club's mid-shift (from four p.m. until midnight), you'll also have one or two mangers working.

Based on club's size & level of class, the staff goes like this:

- In the day (including mid-shift) during the week they'll have between 10 – 15 dancers, one or two bartenders, two bar backs, two or three servers, and three bouncers.
- At night during the week there are 15 – 25 dancers, two to four bartenders, two bar backs, three or four servers, plus three bouncers. Bottle Service and Shot Girls are also part of the servers on the night shift.
- At night on the weekends there are 50 – 75 dancers, four bartenders, three bar backs, four or five servers, and six or eight bouncers. Bottle Service and Shot Girls are also part of the servers on the night shift.
- For big nights or major events at a known spot, there can be 60 dancers or more, plus those clubs will hire off duty city or metropolitan police officers as part of their security detail. All staff members will be there.

Quick Advice: For major events, veteran girls plan ahead by getting hired at another club scheduled to have a celebrity make an appearance. They get in good to make their money, and then leave that club when the event is over.

Some bartenders will allow you to run a tab with them. But pay it as soon as possible because they may get charged for your delinquent bill. Often times, management doesn't know when a bartender is running tabs for dancers, so whatever goes on between the bartender and dancer should remain. You never agitate someone who can help you out in the long run.

Speaking of drinks, like in any club setting, always watch where your drink is because a customer may put something in it. Take your drink with you. If you set your drink down, then went to the rest room or dressing room, when you come back discard the drink you left and order another to be safe.

If a club has a kitchen there's usually one – four people working back there. Clubs with a kitchen that serves decent food are life savers on days you're busy before your shift, or if you're on the go hustling hard on shift. The higher tier clubs have kitchens with a full staff, a refrigerator to put your food in, with few having small luxuries such as coffee or espresso makers. Those with a refrigerator ask for you to help keep it clean, and just about all clubs have a microwave for you to use.

Clubs without a kitchen usually have menus from restaurants near the club you can order from. Some places have food trucks, or people with large portable grills in front of the club. And with far out clubs access to food is limited, so if needed, get someone trustworthy to get you grub and you pay them back.

Managers are the eyes and ears of the owners. They must report and keep track of the money coming in and out of the club, coordinate the safety of the girls and staff, so it's a lot of responsibility. And bouncers are the muscle keeping trouble to a minimum, and the girls feeling safe when they enter and leave the club. Some dancers find either of these two very sexy, so they end up sleeping with one or the other. I strongly recommend you refrain from doing this.

The managers and bouncers that sleep with the girls, more than likely have a significant other. And not only that, from what I've seen, they sleep with or have slept with more than one of the other girls at the club. Some girls grow emotionally attached, and are lied to by these guys who may tell them they're single, separated or leaving their wife for them. And when two dancers in love with the same guy find out about each other, a fight can occur.

Some managers or bouncers will keep trying to get in your pants, but don't be a young and dumb naïve girl. Do not have any sexual relations with anyone on staff. You're there to get money and go, with no strings attached.

Quick Advice: Some managers are sneaky con artists. If a manager is coming up with fines for you to pay that sound outrageous, they probably are. This is a way to pimp you in a roundabout fashion.

More Quick Advice: In lower level clubs and hole-in-the wall spots, a physical or verbal altercation between bouncers, customers, bartenders, and/or dancers can happen at any time. Be

on guard because a loud argument one minute can turn into an all out brawl the next minute, or worse a shoot-out.

As quick advice in the last chapter, I suggested you go to a respected and honest bartender, or server that used to dance for help. Take your time in learning the staff, getting a feel for who is cool and who is trouble. Some of the staff is negative energy you don't need around, and they may even set you up to get robbed so watch who you're dealing with.

House Mothers can play different roles at different clubs. In some clubs she's the manager who does the hiring. And in others she's the woman in a club's dressing room who sells snacks and supplies to the dancers. If you're ever in need of a safe place to stash the money you made that shift, she can be a trustworthy ally.

The second kind of House Mother can be a new girl's safety net. If you're broke and can't afford to get or forgot to bring hygiene products, missed a meal or need a snack, she'll start a tab for you that you must payback as soon as you can. The latter version's fee is mandatory, and the items' costs vary from House Mother to House Mother.

DANCER PERSONALITY TYPES

Some of these dancers fit into multiple sections, but do know you shall encounter all these types in due time. From Dante's Inferno onto a stage near you, the seven types of deadly sinners are among this group. To avoid transgressors of more than one iniquity, memorize who's who and what they do.

Newbies

Newbies (or rookies) are the fresh faces on the club scene. They are under a year in the game, broke all the time, and timid while in the dressing room. Nearly all newbies thought that being a dancer would be easy, but then half of them see it's not for them and leave after a night or two of trying.

If you're a newbie and willing to stay in this game, the best thing to do is shut up and pay attention. Learn your surroundings, and ask questions only after you understand how some people are. If you come in thinking you know everything already, you will make enemies quickly when you don't need to.

Newbies can use this status to their advantage because most guys like knowing they have an innocent thing they can dirty up. A newbie can make a small mint if they know how to play this role well. School girl, secretary, or personal assistant roles are great to play in these situations, for the man feels in control. Have your daddy's little girl persona ready for these types of customers.

The Regulars

These girls have been in this game around two years or more. They have an idea of how to maneuver the club scene, and who not to operate with. Regulars normally come in, say hi & bye, crack a few jokes, but stay focused on getting that money because they got responsibilities. These women are called "Go Getters" as well.

Club Divas

These women are regulars who think they're the sexist women anywhere. They want the spot light on them all the time, and are often conceited, materialistic, and air headed. Many feel since they're beautiful, the world should belong to them. And every one of them thinks they can get or seduce any guy they want.

The biggest gold diggers I ever met were in this bunch. They always bragged about whom they're dating that has money, but they themselves are broke half the time. In my opinion, I think some of them want to be trophy wives, but aren't sophisticated enough to land a man of status.

Divas tend to roam in cliques as if they were in high school again. Fake laughs, fake hair, fake everything, yet they're at each others' birthday parties and hanging out all the time -- gossiping.

O.Gs or Veterans (Vets) or Mascots

These ladies have been in the game seven years or more. They worked in different clubs, and done seen it all and been through it all. A cool down-to-Earth O.G/mascot can guide a newbie away from unnecessary drama. Some of these ladies are in their late 30s and even 40s, who I've danced with at the lower quality clubs.

Many O.Gs never really planned ahead, and got used to being in the life. Some went on to do others things in the club like bartend or even became management. Few finally went back to school and finished then got a normal job like nursing.

Try avoiding being the kind of O.G. that's in-and-out the club scene over the years. The type of veterans with certifications, degrees, a small business, or careers dancing paid for, but they still dance every so often. I know mascots who are grandmothers that returned because they fell on hard times, due to improper planning or overspending. Others are simply too dependent on easy money to let the scene go.

Quick advice: Many of the girls are bi-sexual or bi-curious. Some are beautiful lesbians who use this to their advantage since they aren't into men at all. So be careful because newbies get hounded by dominant lesbians looking to turn them out. Ladies, if you choose to experiment or don't condone lesbianism then ignore the lesbians who approach you sexually. Let them know that no

means no in the best way possible, for dominant lesbians are extremely persistent.

DANGEROUS COMPANY

This lineup of dancers can bring the most woe into your life as a stripper. Their bad habits, sour attitudes, and deceitful actions must be rejected at all times.

Low Class Sluts

Out of all the dangerous girls these are harmless, but their level of professionalism should never be copied. They usually dress like the hood rat/slutty tramp from down the street. They sleep with guys because he's cute, a few hundred dollars is a good week's pay to them, and if they do prostitute themselves it's at a discounted rate. They're just all around basic broads with messy reputations.

In truth, some of these girls because they undercut competition with their prices for dances and other things, this causes rifts between them and veteran dancers. I have seen dancers confront and even beat up a slutty girl because of this.

I've seen veterans tell security and management about what they're going to do to that girl and why. A smarter more level headed manager will reprimand the slut to avoid any fighting. But at the lower end clubs, you better be ready to rumble because those girls have nothing to lose, and no one will help you.

Quick Advice: In case you're wondering, yes these are the type of women who will sleep with your man. Not just guys who are dating co-workers from the club, I mean they will sleep with whoever they think is handsome regardless of relationship status. Do your best at keeping this home wrecker away from any heterosexual male who is of age you care about.

Drama Queens

There's always a girl or two that make enough on some nights for the house fee. Oddly enough, they just sit somewhere around the club, gossiping with customers or other dancers. They'll spread any and everyone's business around the club, regardless of how hurtful. Keep your conversations short or non-existent once you come across these girls.

Say hello to be nice, or if they ask for small things like a stick of gum be courteous, besides that ignore what they have to say. These girls are two-faced toward friends by smiling in their face, then talking trash about them when they're not around. If you're getting attention from a good-looking customer she likes, a Drama Queen will automatically be jealous of you. A lot of times she'll start rumors about you, trying to hurt your grind and receive attention. Some customers enjoy the drama, especially if they're a part, or at the center of the he say-she say nonsense. You and the other girls are there to get money from customers, not tear each other down. So if you hear or see anything gossip worthy, keep it to yourself -- you don't know a thing.

Always avoid customers that enjoy seeing dancers mad at one another. Certain kinds of drama can lead to girls verbal sparring or fist fighting. I've seen girls get sucker punched, and others step to a gossiper, asking them about what was said then started throwing blows. Most gossipers learn their lesson, but as for you reading this, unless you know how to dodge a jab or a wild haymaker, just focus on your money.

Quick Advice: Some girls will try sneaking dances from long time customers of yours, knowing that the customer is a regular while you're on shift. If you see this happening, be diplomatic and approach management. They'll either tell the dancer who violated to be more mindful, or they'll arrange a face to face with the girls to settle the problem. But do note that the customer chooses what they want to do with their money, so don't get angry if he picks another girl.

More Quick Advice: Two dancers can figure a way to get paid from the same guy. Negotiate for the days you're not there, she can get that money from your regular. And if she be so kind to share info on a guy in her clientele base (on the same financial level as your regular) who comes on your days on and her days off. Let her know you don't want to feel cheated or have any animosity, so it's only fair. If she's down for this, let her know what he likes, as she does the same for you. Remember, this is only for that one customer, not your whole clientele base. Plus, make sure the girl is sensible and pragmatic because a selfish or

untrusting dancer may take this as you scheming, and give you faulty information.

Miss Know-It-All

They claim to know all the tricks of the trade, quick to tell you what you ought to do, but don't have anything to show from their great advice. Then when you try to inform them about something, they will state that they already knew, yet they're not practicing what they preach to make money. Unless a person has successful experiences in a field, don't listen to a Mister or Miss Know-It-All.

Lying Chicks

Every member of this group is a pathological liar. They tell big lies like having a kid or not, to little lies such as how they have their hair done. Some liars are really sneaky, for they'll tell you a lie about customers or lie to customers about you, keeping you from making money.

Some dancers take cues from these girls by having a sob story they'll tell customers for when nights are very slow. I've heard lies from girls saying they're close to eviction, to an abusive boyfriend she's trying to leave, to a child suffering from asthma. If you want to use this technique, feel free, but remember that you must keep track of the lies you told, and who you told them to.

Lying dancers lead customers on who they know have fallen for them. They'll tell the guy how they enjoy their company, and make him feel like he can save her, or make the customer feel like she understands him. They'll even shed tears for dramatic effect, so the guy can really open his wallet to help her. These girls really think they're slick.

Quick Advice: Some customers know when a dancer is lying, so they'll just tell her lies as well. Basically, you have two people swapping falsities, playing along with the fantasy. But this can hurt a liar because some customers don't like to be told a bunch of untruth.

They-Need-Help Girls

These women have it hard for they're either mentally unstable (bipolar disorder, schizophrenia, multiple personalities, etc), drug addicts or alcoholics in need of therapy. If you can, get them some help because they're a danger to themselves as much as they are the public. Many of them don't realize they need help, so just keep an eye on them, and play it cool. If they act like they don't want your help, then leave them be until they choose to do so.

Club Bully

The women of this group are mean for no reason. If you ever seen the movie *Players Club*, the character Ronnie best describes this batch of dancers. They'll push around most newbies, doing things such as knocking down or kicking her things just to start a fight.

Some appear nice at first, until you see how deceitful they are because they're trying to pimp or rob you. Most bullies feel they must be in control of that setting for their lives are out of sorts. Tell management about any bullying going on so that girl can be penalized. You're too cute to be fighting silly women.

Money Hungry Crooks

These ladies are deceitful to say the least. All they have is money on their mind and don't care how they get it. They will smile in your face all while setting you up to be robbed. They've set up customers with money to burn, by slipping something in that person's drink. Some have boyfriends who sell dope, and help them move weight (drugs) cross country, while others may overcharge customers for dances.

Be on the look out for women with Visine bottles at ready. Most that slip a Micky in a customer's drink use Visine bottles as their tool of choice. So tell management or if you can, the owner about this so these socio-psychopaths can be dealt with properly.

You don't want to live with the guilt, knowing a girl put too much poison in a customer's drink, then that patron dies all because he wanted to have a good time.

CUSTOMER PERSONALITY TYPES

The main thing to remember is these guys are stepping away from their lives for a few hours. Some will lie about having significant others, kids, and even about their actual professions. You are there to be that dream girl of his. You're there to get his mind off the hustle and bustle, and onto you but for a fee. You're not here to date, or have sex with an attractive man. If you want a new relationship, try online dating, but while you're at the club get paid and get out.

Normal 9 to 5 Guys (Blue Collar Men):

They are usually 28 years old and up, and been in a particular job field for ten years or more, with an established routine. They're either in construction, are longshoreman, mechanics -- just guys who work with their hands.

With the nine to fivers, just introduce yourself nicely, with a smile. Let them know a good honest man is hard to find, especially with the fools that come into the club. Even if they're boring conversationalist, let them feel like their presence is a breath of fresh air every time, as if talking to them is the highlight of your day.

In some introduces you must break the ice. Please brush up on your sports, politics, cars, guns, or agree (even to a certain extent) about things women do that the blue collar guy may bring up. If he likes you at first sight, you won't have to seduce him too hard. But with others you must calm his nervousness by suggesting he get a drink or you get him a drink, letting him know you'll take care of him. Making a man in this group feel like a boss, after his long day or week of work does wonders for your wallet.

Quick Advice: Read or skim every section of your daily newspaper or magazines guys like. Also watch television channels or check websites that interest men. Nothing impresses a guy like a woman they can relate to. Some guys will pay you a few bucks just to talk to them about dude stuff.

More Quick Advice: When talking to a customer, it's cool to act interested in the topic he's discussing. But after 3 or 4 songs (five to ten minutes) of conversing, proposition him for a dance. If they aren't interested, move onto the next customer but be nice about it. Move along but let them know if they need you, you'll be near, or tell them you have a friend to say hi to, or a special customer to check in with as a courtesy.

The Pervs:

Few are young guys, but most perverts are older men in their 40s and older. The old pervs do things like pull out their privates as you're dancing, or touch you very inappropriately like purposely sticking their fingers into one of your lower body cavities. They're normally on the floor waiting for girls they find attractive to get a dance from, or sitting by the stage touching their self as a girl works the pole.

If you encounter one, either ask them politely to put their privates back into their pants and not mess up your special moment, or call security if the bouncer doesn't toss him out already for being repugnant. Pervs aren't easy to spot at first, for they reveal who they are when a girl dances. From my observations, pervs normally wear sweat pants (the cotton kind), or basketball shorts, both without underwear on. Some will also put a hole in the pants front for their penis.

Once again, you can either tell them to tuck it but in a sweet way, or leave then tell security.

Pimps & Macks:

Pimps and Macks either have a girl or more in a club, or they're recruiting for a new girl. These characters aren't hard to detect. A girl or two will address them as "daddy." If a guy or woman approaches you claiming they can upgrade your life, or promises to get you more money and change your lifestyle, leave because they're giving you pimp lines.

Losers:

These bums come to the club with no money. Losers don't buy drinks, don't get dances, or tip any of the dancers. They just hide in a corner, looking at girls and vibe to the music. Some may hold a conversation, seeing if they'll get a dancer's phone number but never gets a dance.

If you spot one, tap security or better yet the DJ about this. Some DJs will put a spot light on the loser in order for him to leave in embarrassment. If you are a male reader, remember, if you ain't got any money stay home. Losers seem to forget that the club is a place of business, so treat it as such.

Ballers:

These guys come in with intensions to spend or throw around a lot of money. Ballers are sports players, entertainers like rappers, singers or movie actors, some are business minded criminals (drug dealers, gangsters), and others are entrepreneurs who had a large win streak. They usually come in around midnight or later. Ballers show up at random, on their night off from work with others who are his friends, or other Ballers looking for a good time. Be careful because many of these men are arrogant, and some have no class at all, thinking because they have money, they can treat people anyway they want.

With Ballers, charm them and congratulate them on their success, but don't laud all over them. Be curious and ask them business related questions like "did you follow a business plan," or "how can I try getting into that field?" Seem like you have plans and other things on the horizon besides what's expected with most dancers. Later in this book, I'll explain how a contact like this may come in handy.

Ballers enjoy being the pursuers. They will either choose a girl to get dances from every time he comes around, and some even date the girls they like. The newbie dancers from meager beginnings often become big headed when a Baller shows them the world, and buys them things. Other times, the Ballers may go after the divas of the club because they're attracted to a boss lady, but only if they appear classy. But be warned, if a Baller is dating you for a while, he may drop you for someone new. Very few women become the wife of a Baller. If anything, you may just be his woman on the side (side piece or mistress).

Quick Advice: If the Baller is a known drug dealer/dope boy, gangster, or a scammer (a person running credit cards, tax refund, checks or other scams), you dance or date him at your own risk. At any given moment, trouble can happen with him being the target in the club, or if you guys are hanging out somewhere. If

you're dating this type of guy and he gets locked up, this is your chance to leave him and move on with your life. Change your phone number and move if you must, but let him know you're not waiting for him while he's away.

More Quick Advice: Ballers who are hanging with the entrepreneurial types may turn their section into a business meeting. If you're ever in these circles, just do what's asked of you until they're done. Be cute and listen in, and if you're smart, you'll get a business card just in case. Business deals or discussions do get done on golf courses, front row at sports games, poker tables, vacation cruises and in clubs more than you think.

Wannabe Ballers:

These guys' flash cash or brag about what kind of car they have, or lie about how they get their money to intrigue you. After a while you'll see that their funds are limited, and probably have child support they aren't paying, still live at their parent's house, or are living beyond their means.

Corporate Men:

The suit and tie guys (both formal and business casual in outfit) normally come in around happy hour. They start off their night by buying drinks for their friends, co-workers and/or clients. Most times they purchase bottles when they're in groups, and more times than not, make more money than the blue collar crowd.

Like the Ballers, corporate guys always want the finer things in life, but they differ in the girls they get dances from. They strictly go after beautiful dime pieces that not only have hot bodies, but also great faces, while Ballers more go for a girl who's cute but not overly pretty with a great body. But be careful, some in this crowd may be looking for a beautiful mistress, so keep it professional and don't date them.

Corporate men do party hard with some being functioning addicts (drug abusers or alcoholics with a job), so don't give into the peer pressure presented. When they arrive, the ones who are married are trying to escape their lives for a few hours, but not get into any trouble, so they'll pay to keep their sneaky business quiet.

Suit and tie guys come in often to celebrate a big business deal, a promotion, a bachelor party, or even a divorce party. They don't want any basic broads around, only classy and sharp women to talk to. So if you have the gift of gab, and is a great sales person with an eye for business, then they'll fall for you.

Like the Ballers, some corporate men will turn the V.I.P section into a meeting room where only the stunning beauties of the club can enter. And also like with the Ballers, just be attentive, and if you can get a business card because you may need their expertise in the long run.

Quick Advice: If you're ever with Ballers or corporate movers you network. Once, a friend of mine went on a 7 day cruise and he told me that he saw well-off corporate guys talk about their sons, and what connections they have. Each of them exchanged business cards and set meeting dates. While all the young and wild folks on the ship were in the club area later that night, the smarter focused young people were in the ball room earlier, networking while on vacation. They say the best deals are usually done on the golf course, so take advantage of the corporate company you're around.

The Hang Outs:

These customers can be confused for the nine to fivers, in part because of how they dress (t-shirt and jeans or shorts). The main difference is that these guys only carry but a certain amount of money to spend that night, usually $40 - $120. They just want to get out the house to hang out for a while to clear their heads. I give them props for they're budgeting money wisely, something that'll come in handy later in this book.

To spot a hang out or a crew of hang outs, see if they are supporting the bar heavily, and how many girls they get dances from. If he gets around five dances from a girl, tip a few dancers and the bartender then he may have $80 to $120 to spend. On a slow night, or if a drought (Droughts are when days up to a couple of weeks things are slow) happens, enough dances from enough hang outs can help you survive.

Be careful because some hang outs are great conversationalist. If you're not paying attention, you and a hang out may discuss your whole life story when you could've been mingling for money. Always keep your conversations short. After a few songs, if he isn't getting a dance, move it along politely.

Crazy Customers:

There are varying degrees of loons that come to the club. Some come in with bad attitudes, bringing their drama from work or home with them to the club. Others are so possessive and clingy to where you think you need a taser on deck at all times.

Angry-crazy customers can be easier to deal with than you think. If they're hostile, let security handle it. If they verbally snap at you, try to calm them down by apologizing immediately. Offer to get them a drink and be sweet about it. Regardless of what happened, let them know the problem may not be their fault, and you'll take care of them if they remain calm.

Just talk with them for a while, and hear them out. Best believe that by being a good ear, can lead to him wanting dances from you that night, or the next time he comes around because you had his back.

If they're angry and drunk then just leave them alone, and let security or management know they may have a problem ahead. In fact, those who arrive to the club drunk are often volatile and rude. Be mindful of those who are enjoying their night while drinking alcohol, from the ones who have a mean spirit about them.

The stalker types are the ones you must spot quickly. These are the guys who may stare at you all night, whether they get a dance or not. If they see you flirting with another customer they might get emotional about it, and some may even approach you as if they're your man. Look, regardless of how much money a customer is willing to spend, if that person creeps you out don't dance for him.

Some crazy guys will overstep boundaries and feel you up during dances, so you better be ready to show some backbone at times, especially in hole-in-the wall clubs. Let them know that if they proceed with the nonsense they will be exited. And if they continue touching anyway, if needed, stiff arm them and then walk away.

Though I've hardly seen corporate men act up like this, crazies are found in all groups mentioned in this section. This is another reason why prostituting or having sexual relations is a dangerous thing in this game. Keep your legs closed and mouth to yourself, for some guys are so lonely and thirsty, once they've had a piece of a woman, he may not want to let it go.

Quick Advice: If you drove to work and feel unsafe, ask security to walk you to your car. Some clubs have a door where they can sneak you out through. Also as you walk to your car, place the keys in your palm and then make a fist over your keys. Have the longest key poking out between your fingers, so if needed, you can stab as you jab whoever jumps out. If you have high heels with spikes, us those as well or just get pepper spray. Always drive different routes every time you leave the club. And make sure your car is in order in terms of how it runs, because you never want it to break down at the wrong time.

More Quick Advice: If you're catching a taxi home, write down the cab's company name, who the driver is, and the cab's car number. Share this info with a manager/house mother, a bouncer, family, friend and/or dancer you know has your best interest. Share a taxi with other girls if you can because there is safety in numbers. And make sure the cab driver understands that as a woman, you must protect yourself at all times -- it's no slight on him.

<u>WARNING</u>

 Always give fake phone numbers or no numbers at all to customers, and always stick to your dancer name. People will look up your name and info on the internet so fast it's shocking. If you're on social media and want to keep to yourself, place your accounts on private. If you have clientele such as a Baller, or those who spend lots of money on you, if truly necessary get a secondary pre-paid cell phone to use strictly for business.

The Needy & Slimy Customer:

These jokers are not to be associated with. These sorry excuses are either trying to sleep with you (Slimy) or scheme money out of you (Needy).

Needy customers are like Wannabe Ballers for they brag about what they don't have, hoping to impress you. They keep trying to sweet talk you, asking if you're single or state how they'll do more for you than your man can. But in the long run, their trying to con you, hoping you'll spend money on them.
Most guys who are Ballers, you can look them up by researching, plus on more than one occasion they'll spend tons of money. With time it shall reveal who's needy so ignore any big money talk.

Slimy customers aim to sleep with you by any means. They'll offer money they don't have for you to date them, tell lies in the form of sweet talk about how he'll help you out and growing something meaningful. But once he gets what he wants, he's never calling you again. The fastest way to spot a slimy one is by hearing how negative his words are toward another dancer. They'll say stuff like "why are you hanging with that dirty girl?" or state how another dancer is low class and trifling.

Sugar Daddies:

Men in this category are around 55 years old and higher, and want to act as an authority or father figure to a dancer. Sugar Daddies look for girls between 18 and 28 years old -- roughly 20 years younger than they are. They usually go after newbies who don't have much, so they can be the one spoiling them. They not only give girls money, but also gifts and even trips around the world.

Not all sugar daddies have a lot of money. Some are on fixed incomes, and others are still working during retirement age. But regardless of whether they have a lot of money or not, treat them with respect and like they matter. Men of a certain age may feel forgotten and need to feel like they still have that 'it' factor.

From my observation, a sugar daddy either:

- Seeks sexual gratification from a dancer.
- Give pretty girls money to flirt and talk with.
- Want a young girl as arm candy when in public.
- Enjoy dealing with very naïve or air headed girls
- Act single though they're married
- Long time serial daters who always took care of a woman
- Loners in need of company.

You will easily come across girls with a sugar daddy in this game. Dancers' who do have them, keep at least three on call, with one go-to-guy who may pay a girl's bills for the month so she won't have to work. They follow his lead because older guys are stuck in their ways, and have a set schedule they never break from.

Quick Advice: Some sugar daddies are possessive because they're spending money on you. I suggest you never date one, or do anything with them outside the club. You don't want a grumpy old dude deep in lust (or love) with you at the club, ready to curse you out.

Captain-Save-A-Hoe:

The save-a-hoe crowd falls under two definitions:

The first kind falls for a girl, and promises to take her out the club to make his wife. If she goes for this, months after moving in with him, the captain will be back in the club looking for a new girl to save. Rarely do any of these relationships last for a long time. Some may last one or two years, but by the third it's over.

Other captains in this first classification, after solidifying a relationship, want you to be a housewife but realize later that they can't provide for you financially. Some will kick the girl out when his money gets low, while others asks' the girl to get a job to help out. If you love him and he's a good man, don't be angry get a job to help out. If he's telling you to leave, then he never loved you, and you don't need him. This is why having money saved from your dancing days can come in handy.

The second type of save-a-hoe is helpful to a dancer on slow nights, and you need money for something important. They'll come in at random an hour or so before last call, and give you exactly what's needed, and then some. Just about every dancer has a "slow night but was saved" story.

Quick Advice: Save-A-Hoes might be abusive (either physically, verbally or both) and very insecure. If you're still dancing, they may show up at the club, and threaten you because you're flirting with a customer, not realizing you must play a role to get money.

Tricks & Johns:

Though most dancers have many financial barriers their facing, I would rather them not sell their body. But some girls out of desperation take a date for a large amount of money. If you feel you can live with this decision may whom you praise be with you. But do know that guilt and disgust can lead to mental break down or worse.

Tricks show up to the club looking to sleep with a dancer for a flat fee. Some are straight to the point while others are courteous when asking if you're that kind of girl. The arrogant tricks are quick to throw money in your face, assuming that every girl has a price. Sadly, most girls get into meeting Johns and turning tricks.

Tricking is something dancers may do once or twice, with others figuring it's easier sticking with whoring for money. If you aren't with this, let the Trick/John know that you're to be respected and if they don't stop negotiating, they can leave. Or if needed, tell them you have someone special who takes care of you at home, and you're not messing that up for no amount of money.

Quick Advice: Unless you're doing a bachelor party or birthday party with other girls, I seriously suggest you never do any private shows at a customer's place. That person may be some weirdo or worse, so don't even think about accepting meet ups with only you and that one person.

Female Customers:

Lady customers are either: bi-curious straight women, lesbians or bi-sexual. With straight girls, they come in to enjoy themselves and support the dancers. They buy drinks, and even get table tops or lap dances from time to time. Some ask dancers questions out of curiosity about dance moves, how long you've been dancing, are certain parts of your body real, or where you got your outfit from.

Some straight girls are dancers from another club, scouting the area, or ex-dancers seeing how the scene has changed. Ex-dancers come in and show love by tipping, or getting dances because they know how hard the grind can be.

The straight girls come in 2 categories though: ones who are hard working 9-to-5 women, and those who are broke and classless. The hard working women are cool, but the classless ones are sometimes in the club flirting with the guys who're spending money. These unsophisticated women are unnecessary competition. They need to be banned from clubs for they interfere with your money, so they can get paid.

Even worse, many of the classless come in judging you, but they're busy looking for tricks in the club. Unsophisticated women are usually loud, obnoxious, and always want to be the center of attention. It is bad enough dancers must deal with other dancers, but the unwanted actions of the classless are an added stress.

When lesbian customers come in, many of them dress and have masculine mannerisms. The ones with decent jobs may pay just as well as any guy customer, and more some times. They like hanging with the guys, and are treated as one if they're with a group of men. Some are cool and just all around pleasant to talk to, so give them a dance if they're paying.

A majority of lesbians who are more masculine in appearance either have a girlfriend who works at the club, or they're looking to sponsor a girl. Some may get aggressive when pursuing a girl, saying things like: "you don't need a man" or "you ever have a woman in your life" or "you don't know if you gay."

With many of them, they try spoiling a woman, buying what that likes. They usually go after inexperienced newbies for they are thought of as easier to turn out.

Lesbians don't want a bi-sexual woman -- they don't want their women being with men period. The bold lesbians have a ton of confidence, and feel they can make any woman become homosexual. And out of curiosity, most dancers give in and try this lifestyle for a while. Though some girls remain this way for years, others feel wrong about it and eventually go back to being straight. Bi-sexual women usually come in with their boyfriends or husbands. They sometimes are with lady friends who don't know they like women as well. They'll try getting your phone number for extra entertainment, but just keep it business as usual or don't do it all.

Quick Advice: Some of the more masculine lesbians can be pimps and macks as well, so be careful. And like with a certain amount of guys, there are lesbians who will cheat on a girl with another woman, so be mindful.

Wives, Lovers & All Significant Others:

Couples come to the club in search of fun and exploration. They go either because the woman is bi-curious/bi-sexual, or want to see why the strip club is the place to be. When they're open and inviting, couples get girls to dance for each other with the women asking dancers questions. It's like a field trip for grown kids.

Watch your step though because dancers often meet guys who don't talk about their wife, girlfriend or crazy baby mama. The guy's lover may mistake you for the dancer he's cheating with, and try fighting you. If this occurs, try evading the woman, and let security do their job because you're too pretty for all that nonsense.

These guys are very charming and are great at learning what you like, but remember to never date a customer. It can be bad for business and even your well-being. Even if he is single, making him your man can be the wrong move.

Quick Advice: I'll tell you about a dancer who came in on her night off. She was tall, slim, and had a nicely shaped rear end that was round and toned – you can never forget her. I guess she was supposed to be home because her crazy boyfriend came to the club, and escorted her to his car. I made my quota for the night, so I decided to leave early. As I walked by the two sitting in his car, I heard him yell at her. When I looked to see what was going on, I witnessed the guy banging that woman's head into the dashboard. Security heard the whole thing, but nobody helped because the guy was a known criminal. After 30 more seconds of his assault, he started up the car and sped off. The girl came back on her regular work night a few weeks later. This time whenever that guy called her cell phone, she knew to be ready when he came through and she stayed home when he said so. Enjoy dating sociopathic or psychopathic customers at your own risk.

CHAPTER 4:
DRESS, MOVE & SEDUCE

So you think you're cute?! Yeah, maybe you know how to shake your butt at a house party, and twerk or prance and strut around a bit. But can you proceed in a way that entices a man into wanting you, and only you out of many beautiful girls? The stuff in this chapter shall separate the slutty girls with rudimentary motions, from the enchantresses who keep customers coming back for more. And ladies, use some of these suggestions on your man, but only if he's been good.

Your main goal is to provide a type of fantasy for every customer. Some guys are lonely, and others are with nagging women who boss them around. They're trying to avoid them for the night, so seeing you must feel like a blessing every time. The art of the tease has been forgotten, therefore never taught to the new girls coming in.

Before the gentleman's clubs, burlesque shows in theater houses were the place to be from the late 1800's all the way to the

1960's. Back then, morals were high, so performers worked the teasing aspects, as well as their sensuality to draw in big crowds. Every girl had their niche and an act, but they didn't have to be fully nude to get men interested. A dancer's creative mind can get her further than flashing breasts and making her rump clap.

The first thing men notice with all women is how we look. A man must be smitten or interested at first sight. He may not be cute to you, but if you look hot enough for him to give you the cash for your car note, then you better have your appearance on point.

Hair:

Make sure your hair is clean and styled in a way that compliments your unique beauty. Don't get a hairstyle based on what you think looks good because not every style is for everybody. There are girls who look like runway models in a certain hairstyle, but look like a bloody banshee in others. So get an honest hair dresser, or talk with someone truthful enough to tell you what will work, and won't work for you.

Face:

Some dancers are naturally gorgeous, and only need their eyebrows arched and apply lip gloss or lipstick. Others must apply makeup for that extra oomph by hiding blemishes. Of course, a dancer shouldn't overdo the makeup process because you don't want to look like a circus clown. Plus you never want your makeup running while you're on stage dancing and sweating, for it can get on a customer's clothes.

If you've never applied makeup, take these basic pointers:

- Get a foundation or liquid foundation that is one shade darker than your skin tone.
- Second is to get face powder that is one shade lighter than your complexion.
- Next, place the foundation on your face first then let it sit for about twenty seconds before applying the face powder.
- Lastly, you mix them together onto your skin, blending them in slowly.

Quick Advice: Thanks to the internet, there are people on YouTube who are masters when it comes to makeup. I suggest looking at tutorials by transgendered women or men who cross dress. I've seen guys make them selves look just as good or better than most women I've danced with.

Body:

Get your manicure and pedicure often, but don't go overboard with how you paint your nails. I suggest you get a simple French Tip design, but if you want to get colors, use as few colors as possible.

Always bath or shower at least twice a day, especially before you hit the dance floor. Even if you must take what some girls call a "bird bath" (where one washes their neck, arm pits, under the breasts, vagina and then booty), staying fresh is part of the seduction. People always remember how a person looked and smelled.

Keep in your dancer bag a small bar of soap or body wash, and a washrag. Some of the nicer clubs have showers or restrooms in the dressing room. For the ones that don't have, if you must, use a restroom sink in the floor bathroom where the customers utilize.

Your dancer bag must have at all times:

- ➤ Soap and washrag
- ➤ Toothbrush
- ➤ Toothpaste
- ➤ Mouthwash
- ➤ Baby wipes
- ➤ Feminine wipes
- ➤ Deodorant
- ➤ Body spray
- ➤ A pair of sneakers
- ➤ 2 pairs of heels
- ➤ Different costumes or lingerie with bottoms (bottoms are g-strings, thongs, boy shorts, etc.)
- ➤ Hair brush
- ➤ Garter belt & rubber bands
- ➤ A CD or flash drive with your musical selections
- ➤ And a money bag for your cash on good nights.

Quick Advice: A money bag can be the size of a Crown Royal bag or a clutch purse. When you're having a great night, you'll need this to keep your tips and dance money safe. Remember, if the club has a locker room, never share a locker and always have your own lock just in case. If a club doesn't have lockers, if you must, give your money bag to a manager but count the money with him before handing it over.

More Quick Advice: Always present yourself like a lady. When stepping into the club, do not have on head scarves, bedroom slippers, hats, hair rollers, or look like you just cleaned house or did laundry. Have on a nice casual outfit for day shift, and dress like you're heading to a dance club for night shift. Customers must see you at your best at all times, so make your first impressions your best impressions.

House Mothers and some managers as stated earlier have many things a dancer needs, including tampons. Be nice with her because no one likes a girl who begs and borrows all the time, especially when people know she has the money to get it herself.

Along with not using a lot of makeup, don't put body glitter or perfume on your skin. If you use body spray, just put a light amount because some guys aren't supposed to be at the club, so don't get your customer in trouble with his lady. For those who want to use lotion, apply it at least five hours before your shift. Lotion, baby oil, and gels can make the pole and certain spots on stage a dangerous work hazard waiting to happen, so avoid using them while on shift.

After dancing on the pole or for two – three customers on the floor, go in the dressing room to wipe and wash yourself, even if you think you don't. Be mindful that you're moving around a lot -- basically doing a cardio workout. I suggest that dancers should wash or wipe their rear ends, vaginal areas, arm pits, and under their breasts every 30 minutes to an hour.

Clubs usually have a bottle of rubbing alcohol, but if you can, have alcohol and hand sanitizer at all times. You use the rubbing alcohol to wipe down the pole before starting your set. Baby wipes will be your best friend because toilet tissue bits aren't sexy, especially if any rubs off onto a customer. And for those who work in an all nude club, it's wise to trim down or make smooth your pubic region. Too much hair down below isn't sexy to many men, so regularly shave or wax.

When Aunt Flow Is Around

Girls starting off who are badly in need of money, if you must work during your period, please pay very close attention for you're taking a risk.

Memorize these tips:

> ➤ If your menstrual flow is light then use a light tampon, and change tampons every two hours. If it's a heavy flow, then

use two heavy duty tampons at once, placing them side by side, changing them every hour and a half (90 minutes).

➤ Use soap and washcloth when cleaning yourself after every tampon change. Be sure to also wash your hands when you're finished.

➤ Please do not use baby wipes to clean yourself when on your period.

➤ Always check for smells, and wear dark colored underwear and costumes.

➤ Don't have any alcoholic drinks because blood will pour out of your body faster.

➤ I've seen dancers get creative when in tough situations as this. Some girls instead of a tampon or pad, they used cotton balls and others utilized face makeup sponges.

➤ Whatever you use, never flush these items down the club's toilet. Always dispose of these items by placing them into the trash, and never letting them fall onto the floor. If you can, please wrap them up in something before tossing them away. Leaving bloody tampons or other items all over the restroom floor, especially ones' customers use make the club look bad.

I strongly urge against working when on your period. It's not sanitary, and if you fail at this attempt, you risk pissing off a customer. So keep track of your menstrual cycle. If you can, just stay home until your period is finished.

Quick Advice: All of this should be common sense, but common sense isn't too common. Always stay fresh by washing your body properly. Some girls have model looks and a million dollar body, but smell like musky gym clothes. They didn't bathe before their shift, sprayed on perfume or body spray, and used baby wipes on their private areas as they danced all night. This isn't sexy, and you can lose money by not being up to par in the hygiene department.

Clothes

You better get comfortable wearing heels because it's part of the uniform. The minimum height for high heels is three inches. If you're not used to wearing them, start by practicing how to walk around in them at home. Clubs will let a new dancer pass if the heels are only two inches. With time increase the height, until you're ready because you don't want to fall and hurt yourself.

For newbies, they probably can't afford the custom costumes the more seasoned dancers get. So I suggest going to adult novelty shops, and getting the $15.00 - $25.00 costumes or lingerie to start with. At the least, you can get booty shorts and bikini outfits from Walmart, Target or the Flea Market, but style it in a way that doesn't look trashy. Using some creativity can get you started off nicely.

Dressing like a low class slut, and not a sexy siren can turn off a customer. A customer doesn't want the whore from up the block, so don't give off that impression. Girls who are in demand will not associate with you, which can be bad for your money. Feature dancers find ways to set themselves apart so take a few pointers from them. Just don't go broke doing so which I'll explain later.

I recommend having at least six costumes or pieces of lingerie to change into during your shift, once you get the hang of it all. How a dancer styles their costume is up to the dancer. Unless the club is having a special occasion where dancers must wear something requested, you can sport whatever you want. For newbies, you may not have the budget for this yet, so try with three or four good outfits then work your way up. Seasoned girls eventually get custom made costumes from women who offer to make them. These outfits range from $125, on up to over $1,000 if the dancer is very well known, or really wants to make a scene.

Some dancers love doing wardrobe changes every hour while on shift just for fun, but it also serves purpose hygiene wise as well. As stated earlier, all this movement and pole work is a workout that you're doing. Eventually bacteria, funk, and stains accumulate while on shift. So be sure to thoroughly wash your costumes every week. Wearing a dirty costume can lead to skin damage such as bumps, acne, rashes or worse.

Quick Advice: When with a customer or on stage, the art of the tease helps tremendously. Taking off your top or everything too soon may not entice your intended targets, which can lead to lower tips and less dances. If you pace yourself, and playfully show the patrons proper eye contact, while flirting with them, anticipation can be built. Make them pay to get each article of clothing off you. Let them know you're body isn't a free show. Let their imaginations work them up so they can tip you more.

The Way You Move

To the newbies, don't worry too much on how you move, that will come in time. For now, get comfortable being on stage in front of people, and learning how to work with customers. Even if you're nervous, just get up there and earn respect. Some girls get scared and opt out from going on stage.

Each time a dancer opts out from going on stage during their shift, you'll be fined $10 to $30 depending on the club. Doing this at a slow time can hurt you. **Example:** Let's say that you made $100 that night. House fee is $30, plus another $30 because you chose not to dance that night. Now let's say on this same slow day, the House Mother collected $10 you owed her from the day before, plus you need to put $15 on the gas tank so you can get around for the next two – three days. That extra $30 could've filled your gas tank, not to mention whatever tips you could've made that night. Don't shoot yourself in the foot, get on stage and make your money.

Quick Advice: Dancers may get a stiff drink to relax them selves before going on stage. One drink that isn't heavy with alcohol is okay, but don't get inebriated. If you can't handle your liquor, you can fall and get hurt, or even throw up on a customer. Plus you're not thinking clearly or paying full attention when intoxicated, so drink lightly. And if a customer gets you a drink, ask for water because it's safe and good for you.

Before getting on stage, the DJ or manager places your name on the DJ list. This is to keep track of whose going on stage and when. They may place you on the list based on who came to work first or who was dressed first -- ready for the floor. Clubs usually ask for the house fee around this time, so have your money ready.

When you're on stage, here are the basics:
➤ As you make your way to the pole, sway side to side with your hips.
➤ Learn to work the crowd with your eyes, and locate the ones tipping you.
➤ Be sure to whine and roll your waist as you lean your back against the pole, using it as a prop in your one woman show.
➤ Dip and bob, up and down the pole every so often, as you seductively circle it.
➤ Lick your lips, blow kisses and wink at those who lock eyes with you, especially if they're tossing money.
➤ If you're near the one giving money, flirt with them as you take what's yours.
➤ Flash a sneak peak of your breast, if it's early in your set, to the person who tipped nicely.

➢ After each song, you remove an article of clothing until you are at the club's set legal limit.

Booty Magic:
There are other ways to make your butt do tricks. Some girls are naturals, while others must practice until they are skilled. Here's one way to go about it. Normal women can try this at home even if they only have a little bit of booty.
1.) Bend over from the waist, and stick your behind out with a slight arch in your back.
2.) While bent over, lean forward against the pole, table, or chair then slightly bend you knees.
3.) Stand on the ball of your feet then swing your heel from side to side, as if you're clicking your heels together.
4.) It'll take some practicing, but when done correctly, you'll be able to make your booty cheeks clap together. It may not clap loudly, but how it moves and jiggles is what counts with customers or your man.

Some girls won't help you, but if you want to learn new moves, talk to the veterans or that one friendly dancer you get along with who's a regular. See how they make they're bottoms jump, gyrate, and clap. With pole work, in all honesty, you can either learn by watching, asking, and then trying things little by little. Or you can click on YouTube, and pick up tips from there because there are dozens of videos about pole work that I wish I had when I first started.

I say after six months or so, you should be ready enough to try a few tricks you learned along the way. Remember, if you don't feel you have the arm, leg, and body strength for risky moves then don't do it. You must build muscle and strength before you can do anything that requires the lifting up of your own body weight.

Quick Advice: Along with a healthy diet, doing calisthenics (pushups, pull-ups, dips, etc.) and working out with light weights but heavy repetitions, plus pole work on the job can help you stay fit. Go to your doctor, and if they approve, get a trainer because the healthier you are, the better you'll look and the more you could do on stage.

When in the club, if you're more of a floor dancer type, smile a lot. Have a seductive grin on your face, if possible. If called over, or you lock eyes with a customer, be flirtatious. Act naïve if you can, and try to give them a cute pet name like "boo," "daddy," "honey bunny," whatever works. If they seem amused by your choice of pet name be playful and ask, "Why you act like you don't want me calling you that?" After that, charm them into a conversation then a dance.

You will come across an angry or rude customer eventually while on the floor. The best thing to do is walk away. If you're always cursing out or physically attacking (punching or slapping) a customer, you can be fined or fired depending on the club. So keep a cool head, and let security do their job.

During any conversation with a customer, if you're talking with them face to face, lightly rub on his shoulder after he introduces himself. If a customer is sitting down, and he engages you, sit in his lap until the next song if he wants a dance. While waiting for the next song, or having him warm up to you, ask questions about whatever subject the customer is talking about. If needed, whatever previous general topic you remember discussing with another customer can be a way to strike up small talk, which often leads to him wanting dances from you.

When you're working at a certain club, after a while you'll begin recognizing who's a regular club patron and who shows up every now and again, from new faces in the place. Learn how to interact with them all. With long time patrons, you'll know whether they like you or not, and with the every-so-often group, when you get a chance, mingle then offer a dance.

Approach new comers with a smile like the gracious hostess you are. A good opening line, especially if it's a group of new comers: "Hi, welcome to (name of the club)…I'm (fill in your name) and I'm part of the welcoming committee. Anything you need, just let me know, I'm here for you (fill in pet name)…What's your name?"

Seduction

When performing a dance for a customer, you must get a sense of whether their enjoying it or not. If the person is unresponsive, it's a strong chance they won't ask for another dance. But if he's enjoying how you move and feed his ego with your sultry words, then keep on dancing. Eventually, if you're doing your job right, you'll see or feel their level of arousal from their erections.

Upon discovery of a hard-on, be classy yet naïve in how you react. Ask things like, "are you enjoying yourself (<u>fill in pet name</u>)?" After asking, increase the teasing by either abruptly getting up from a lap dance, or stopping your table top. Next, lean in so you can tell him, while keeping eye contact, "oh no bad boy, none of that."

Soon after, plant yourself in his lap, or go back to doing your table top, but this time add more eye contact. If you can, compliment him by embellishing the size of his package, but sound convincing by increasing the sultriness in your tone. Add some light moans as if their erection is the best thing you've seen all day. Be sure to whisper in his ear "do you like that daddy?" If he's a new customer, add more sweet nothings in his ear to really make him feel special.

When the song is done, see if they wish to continue. If so, keep dancing or suggest you take it to the champagne room. Use your best customer service skills by not going away right after a song is done. Ask them what else can you do for them? If they don't want anymore dances, thank them for supporting the naked hustle. Be sure to let them know if they need anything, you'll be close by.

Quick Advice: Some guys like getting dances from different girls until they find one they like. Don't anchor yourself by sitting in a customer's lap after doing your dances. You're stopping the flow of other dancers' money, and those girls may not like that. Find another customer and be thankful for the money you did get.

While dancing a customer, whine your waist and say things that may have him drooling over you, but remember to keep it clean as possible. Some clubs don't allow customer's touching so follow the rule. I can't stress this enough how if you begin rubbing on their genitalia, if cops raid the club and that same customer is a cop, he may take you in for disorderly conduct with solicitation. Strip clubs do often get raided every three – six months, so be mindful of the rules.

So while giving a dance be sweet, but if he's crossing the line by trying to rub your vagina, keep calm and tell them to stop or get security. Guys will fondle your breasts or slap your rear end -- that's all part of the game. But them trying to suck on your nipples, grab, finger or touch your genitalia is just nasty. You can be polite yet sexy when telling them to stop by saying things like: "I want to turn you on baby don't turn me off" or "I know you want this, but play nice baby, watch your hands."

After a few dances, a customer may want to go into the champagne room. In upper class clubs, before going into the room, you tell them the price and collect your money. The prices you tell the customers are based on how much the club will get from your champagne room dances. For thirty minutes in the champagne room, a club may suggest you charge $100, and take a $50 cut from you. In situations like this charge the customer $200, and if they want an hour, then charge $300. In lower class clubs, just say a price and pray they have it, if not then negotiate.

PROTECT YOUR HEART

There will be a customer or two whose company you'll enjoy while at the club. He gets dances from you constantly, and through months or years of conversations, you guys may eventually grow a bond. Most likely the customer will catch feelings before you do, but if you can, do not let your heart overtake your commonsense. Regardless of how nice they seem, or how honest he sounds, he's still a customer. He's there to help you pay your bills, and get your life right. Only a very small few of these relationships work, I can't stress this enough.

Some girls let the promise of money and love, dictate who they're dating. They'll be in a relationship with a guy who works hard, that's a blue collar kind of guy, but then meets a guy who's a Baller or a Wannabe Baller. Since the Baller or Wannabe Baller is spending money on her, doing things to sweep her off her feet, she actually gives in, leaving the blue collar guy broken hearted.

I say 98.9% of these situations never end well. The Wannabe Baller eventually shows he's living beyond his means, and is really broke as hell. While the Baller may have more than one woman around, be very controlling & jealous, or dumps you for someone new. Then after you end things, or they dump you, more than likely, the good blue collar guy you left, moved onto someone else.

PROTECT YOURSELF

Some guys who are Ballers in the criminal world are the worst control freaks. Let me give you an example of what I mean. Years back during the early 2000s, I remember a beautiful girl who was dating a known dope man with a wicked temper. Not only was she beautiful with a great smile, tall and tone like a college volleyball player, but she had the perfect hour glass shape. Her boobs were the size of coconuts, and her legs and rear-end were something you would find competing in a Miss Bum Bum competition in Brazil.

Long story short, the dope man used to beat on her during their whole relationship. He was almost like a gorilla pimp towards her because after roughing her up, he'd sometimes tell her to "go make my money." For one reason or another he got locked up for a few years. He told her that she better not be dating while he was away in jail. About a year later, word got to him about her dating a new guy.

On the day he got out of jail, the dope man went to the club the girl was dancing at. He located her near the bar and stabbed her. She went to the hospital, and he fled the scene. Sad to say although she didn't die, about a year later she had the dope man's baby. I left that club months after she had the baby, but ran into her recently. She told me she had two more kids from that crazy man, and how he was doing time for some other petty drug charge. As she spoke, I just stood there thinking *some people never learn*.

Quick Advice: At times you'll talk with a customer about their day, being there when they needed an ear. But as soon as you go to the dressing room to wipe down, or use the restroom, another dancer ends up getting dances from the guy. You may get angry because your 20 minute or more conversation, set things up for another girl. Remain calm, and know next time, don't spend too much time talking. Always be ready to smooth your way into their wallets.

Just being aesthetically pleasing only gets you but so far -- you need to map out how to get some one paying you for your time. How you look catches their eye. How you move brings them into wanting more; and the way you utilize seduction tactics keeps them customers for years at a time. Take what I suggest here, and add your own twist to it. A solid foundation is needed to build great clientele. As time progresses pay attention to the go-getters because they're the ones who make the most money, and search for different ways to reach their goals within club. Be a go-getter, and you'll never go wrong.

CHAPTER 5:
PRIORITIES &
MONEY MANAGEMENT

In the Hip-Hop world, getting your money right is essential to making moves. But in order to accomplish certain goals, one must first learn how to stack money, save for what's important and invest wisely. I've seen many women squander money, left with stories of the good ol' days when they were young and beautiful. Women who saw hundreds of thousands, in some cases millions of dollars throughout their stints as dancers, reach their 40s with nothing to show.

In all honesty, I feel a girl should be in the dancer game at minimum three months with five years being the maximum. Any longer, then you screwed up somewhere. For those dancing in their late teens or early 20s, if you can't exit in the suggested timeframe, then leave before reaching age 30. Those who started in their mid to late 20s, make age 32 the extreme cutoff point, especially if you have kids.

There are situations with women who started off at top notch spots, later ending up in a lower dive bar, dancing with girls old enough to be their daughters. That's right. Now take 30 seconds to let that thought sink in deeply before proceeding.

It's easy to become fully dependent on this business, but this job isn't meant to be a career so get that out of your head. In my eyes, you're supposed to treat it like the drug business, where you come in, figure out the ropes, save your money for something important then leave. This part of the book is dedicated to helping you start on getting out this game, so pay close attention.

STACK YOUR MONEY

As you learn to work a room as well as the stage, and how to get and keep clientele, you must build up the mind frame of a squirrel. What I mean is, like a squirrel you must collect what's needed for the future. Every time you step into the club have a set money goal you must attain. Always aim high with your money amounts because if you aim low, or are content with barely making a few dollars, then you aren't trying to get paid.

During your first few months, if your shifts are normal or fast paced, try reaching a $500 minimum goal, especially if you're on the night shift. Once you get better at dancing and mingling, aim for bare minimum $1000 and higher. In slow times, see if you can get $300 - $400 and higher. But at all times you must think big and go high when it comes to getting money.

In the first three to six months of improving your skills, and the money starts coming, if possible, open a bank account. Try having a *checking* account for normal activities such as paying bills, buying food, and other expenses. The other account will be *savings* where you'll put money away for emergencies, retirement after leaving the exotic dance business, and investing.

Before signing up to a bank research the establishment. See if there are any scandals with that bank, or are they later merging with another institute. Look up the different fees and penalties each possess, and also seek banking alternatives such as credit unions. Whatever works in your favor, do it.

The smart dancers, after getting their accounts, debts and lives on track, compartmentalize their money. With the first $100 - $150 earned on shift, put that toward your house fee for that day and/or tomorrow. Also, with that first $100 - $150, after separating money for tip out, buy food if you didn't bring any from home, put gas in your car or keep it for cab fare -- anything to survive that shift or the next.

Quick Advice: If you know how to cook for yourself, it's best to buy groceries and prepare meals. In the long run you'll save more, and have a healthier waistline in case you land a good man. Also, get a 64 oz. – 72 oz. (1.89 L – 2.12 L) reusable water bottle too. You won't believe how much you'll save monthly by not spending so much on individual 16 oz. – 20 oz. (0.473 L –

0.591 L) bottles water from the store. Even if you only spend $3.00 a day on bottles of water, it comes up to $15.00 every five days which is $780.00 a year.

More Quick Advice: Clip coupons for the things you want when ever you can. Use free gift cards, online deals, or inside hook ups -- take advantage of getting more value out of your dollars. Others may crack jokes about you being cheap, but at least you know you're getting what you want and not breaking the bank for it.

Any money you get after that initial $100 - $150, place them into either your checking or savings account. You'll most likely pay day-to-day priorities from your checking account. With your savings, don't touch that until it's time to make a move, or if you really have a serious emergency. Try telling yourself, "If I make it fast, I must save it fast." With this veteran insight, you'll never be behind, especially if you've been in more than six months.

Quick Advice: Stay away from credit cards unless you plan on building credit. Only use credit (buying a car, getting a home, starting a business, etc) or get a credit card, unless you're going to pay off the complete balance after each use, as fast as you can. Having cash is good, but credit goes an extra long way in America. Before using your credit, I suggest taking a class, reading a book, and/or check a few personal finance videos online first. Understand how credit works and how it can hurt you. I recommend reading *Credit Management Kit for Dummies*, *Increase Your Financial I.Q.* by Robert Kiyosaki, and Getting Loaded: Make a Million…While You're Still Young Enough to Enjoy It by Peter Bielagus.

More Quick Advice: If your credit is already bad, don't worry, you can fix it. First, read information on fixing your credit. Second, draw up a game plan, or speak with a financial advisor with a great reputation to help you draw up a realistic game plan.

Understanding your wants and needs are two things you must know. *Wants* are things you get that are for your pleasure like new jewelry, an expensive meal at a five star restaurant, a $2000 coat, etc. *Needs* are things that are vital to you such as water, shelter, food, clothes and shoes (doesn't have to be name brand), etc. You must keep these in mind for when a drought happens.

Survive the Drought

A slow night can unexpectedly become a slow week or two. Don't panic, it's not the end of the world, but you must hustle hard and be frugal in spending. If you planned on buying a new costume or some other want, place it at the bottom of your list of priorities. Only focus on your bills, and putting whatever you can into your savings. When droughts occur, keep in mind that your money can come from anywhere. You may get $50 from the stage, $100 on the floor with another $150 from the V.I.P. But do know there is more than one way to reach your goal.

You must be like a hawk during a drought, scanning for customers who come in, stay and are actually spending money. You must swoop in before another girl tries charming him. The best hunting weeks to save up for next month's bills are during the second and third weeks of a month. From the 20th all the way until the end of a month, things will get busy.

In those last 10 – 11 days of every month, the club will be packed with girls trying to pay next months rent, which is often due on the first of the month. By you being at least a week early, you don't have to worry about staying on top of your rent/mortgage and bills. Competition is fierce, so be diplomatic in how you interact with other girls in the second half of each month.

Quick Advice: No matter how slow it gets on shift, never leave early, unless you truly must. Clubs charge girls $25 - $50 fines for leaving early. The fee goes up if you don't pay, and decide to do it again. If anything, for emergency reasons, have I-must-go money where you pay the fee then leave.

ON NIGHTS LIKE THIS

On fast nights when the club gets packed, a regular who's about her money scans for: dudes popping bottles; how many people are in an entourage buying bottles as well; and how much money are they converting into $1's. This is crucial because not only will these guys tip or pay well if they like you, but future clientele can come from these groups also. So sit near the V.I.P section or the bar and listen out, for if you're friendly to the right guy, your rent, electric bill and car note can be paid off in one night.

In this world, a good night can bring in $1000 or better. You will get a bunch of single dollar bills, so what you do is convert those singles into bigger bills. Some clubs call it "dollar exchange" or "cashing out", but it reduces the amount of space dollar bills take up. Also, never let another girl or customer know what you made because some fool may rob you. And with carrying money on a garter belt or on your person period, keep your big bills underneath or rolled in between your single dollar bills.

Quick Advice: On good nights, before leaving for home, figure out a clever way to stash your money. If you can, have someone pick it up from you an hour or so before your shift ends.

A girl who's been in the game 18 months or more should have automatic clientele who enjoys her company.

At minimum automatic clientele consist of:

- Three sugar daddies spending $200 - $300, with a main one paying $500 or more on time every week
- Two corporate guys
- 8 - 12 blue collar guys that you change up every other week
- If you can land a Baller you're lucky, so enjoy the ride.

On fast nights, if you see another dancer getting paid, receiving more attention than you, don't get mad or be jealous. Never hate on another girl, just learn to step your game up. Find newer moves, workout more and eat better, so you can have better performances. Always congratulate women who are winning because winners only roll with or respect other winners. That night was her night, the next night may be yours.

Quick Advice: Some people, regardless of how down-to-Earth you may be, will never get along with you. Remember, these are your co-workers and close associates, not your friends. You don't have to like them -- just like the money. If you make a genuine friend in this business, that'll be very rare.

There's a timeframe some veteran dancers call "The Season," where clubs make the most money. The Season starts from mid-October and ends around April 20th of the following year. The Season is so lucrative that women with degrees and decent careers, who danced in the past, come back just to work during that six month stretch for side money.

I suggest you do much more saving than spending during this time. If you make $10.00, save $6.00 or $7.00 bucks, and live on the rest. **For example:** If your monthly expenses are around $3000, but every month during The Season you pull in around $10,000. Live within your means by saving $6000 - $7000 per month of that money, for your way out. $6000 x 5 seasons = $30,000, and this is not including the months afterwards.

HEADING OUT-OF-TOWN

After a year or more working at a particular club, or splitting time between two clubs, promoters and managers take notice of the go-getters. This is a good because it shows you're serious about getting money, which leads to you working outside of your city.

Reputable club promoters may work with many clubs, or event coordinators in different states and/or other countries. Even some of the girls who work in different cities have out-of-town connections for you to get cross country funds. These can be promotional events for a club; a bachelor party; a coming out of jail party; a going into jail party; a divorce party; a business or special organization's shindig; or a yacht or mansion party.

Promoters:

Depending on the events and the amount of events booked for the trip, you can pocket between $1500 - $3000 and better. If times are slow at the club you're at, and you need the funds, these trips come in handy. But before you pack your bags, first ask the other girls who've been out-of-town about the promoter.

Promoters for out-of-town work usually come to a club, and start asking the girls face to face whether they want to do an event or not. It's best to only do this with promoters known at the club you're at. Talk to the managers, so someone other than your family and sister dancers know where you're going. Give them a number to reach you at just in case.

If the promoter isn't known to the club, it's a very risky move. I've been in or heard of situations where the promoter tries leaving without paying you. I've heard of girls being left stranded, while other shady promoters try overworking dancers by booking more events than what they agreed upon. If you roll the dice on a promoter unknown to the club, bring emergency funds for a ticket home just in case.

A good promoter should pay for your room and board, plus travel expenses. They must have quality transportation to and from the event, and security keeping you safe. The only thing you're supposed to pay for is food, refreshments, souvenirs, and emergency money.

Quick Advice: Before going out of town, pay all your monthly bills before leaving. You never want to play catch up when you return home.

TAKE YOUR DRUNK ASS HOME

Regardless of where you are, try not to drink any alcohol or use drugs. When you're out-of-town anything can happen, so keep your wits about you. You never want to be far from home in case things go wrong. In fact, I'll give you an example of how bad being a drunken stripper can be.

A girl I used to partner up on stage with sometimes came to work angry. She spent much of the night drinking heavily. Her boyfriend at the time, who was already high, came in and started yelling at her. They were both asked to leave, so she got dressed and left with him -- both fussing at one another.

I'm not sure who drove, but I know they fought while on the road. They some how lost control of the vehicle and crashed into a gas station. If it wasn't for a few good Samaritans pulling them out the car, they would've been blown up by the gas pumps which caught fire minutes after impact.

Dancing in other Countries

International trips are great experiences you wouldn't want to pass up. I've been to the Bahamas, U.S. Virgin Islands, Puerto Rico, Jamaica, and Mexico -- man I've traveled. Promoters that do international events always go after women who are not only great dancers and good with people, but are physically gorgeous as well. International events are usually big clubs or parties, with people eager to spend big bucks on a pretty girl like you. They are great places to network for future purposes, and the international promoter usually pays for everything including food.

The cool thing (depending on your situation), if you're single, they can keep you working with them for two weeks up to a month or more. So if you want to get away for a while, these out of country gigs are not only profitable, but are also extended vacations. Be sure to keep your paperwork and important travel documents in a place only you know about. Some girls trust the promoter with their information, but don't do this because the promoter will try keeping you on longer than you want. Plus, you never know when you must make an emergency exit home.

Other Girls

Some dancers you meet are known to travel for their money. They'll know a promoter or club manager looking for girls, especially those who are exotic looking and outgoing. Miami, Los Angeles, New York, Atlanta, Las Vegas, Chicago, and even spots in South Carolina have clubs where you can make a nice chunk of change. I've seen girls who barely made $300 on a fast night come back with $2000 in one weekend, so there are many upsides.

Before committing to this trip ask the girl about the venue (whether it's an upscale or lower end club), what kind of money you stand to make, how much is tip out, is it a floor or stage friendly environment. You ladies must figure out the travel arrangements (whether you all are getting a rental together or separate), the cost of the hotel, and other things a promoter would take care of.

The smarter regulars, who've been in this game at least two years that travel, try setting up trips around major events.

Functions you really want to plan for are:

- ❖ NBA All-Star Weekend
- ❖ the Super Bowl, NBA Finals, MLB World Series and NHL Stanley Cup Finals
- ❖ NCAA basketball or football championships
- ❖ Daytona Bike Week
- ❖ Memorial Day Weekend in Miami or Black Bike Week in Myrtle Beach for the more urban scene
- ❖ Las Vegas is usually year round, but major fight nights are better
- ❖ Mardi Gras in New Orleans
- ❖ Well-known college rivalry games, ex. Ohio State versus the University of Michigan

Quick Advice: For nationally recognized events, make your reservations no less than six months in advance. Don't wait until the last minute because it takes time saving money for a trip. Anytime below three months when planning is a horrible idea.

More Quick Advice: Even if you don't like one of the girls on the trip, y'all must stick together. You will get into bitter discussions, but you ladies are a team until you get back home. Y'all came together, so y'all leave together, simple as that.

WHERE THE PARTY AT?

From time to time, you will be asked to do an event at a house, timeshare, or large hotel suite in your city. Be it a bachelor party, birthday, or coming home from jail celebration, these are ways to make quick money. Usually these events are offered to you by management, another dancer, a promoter, or a bouncer looking to make side money.

There are different ways of doing this and all prices are negotiable, but from what I know an upfront fee is paid before a girl even steps foot into the party. This can range from $200.00 to $350.00 per girl. After that, depending on who setup the party, an hourly rate gets placed onto the tab, which ranges from a few hundred dollars an hour up into the thousands.

When you go to the party, one side of the place is for you and/or other girls to dance in front of paying customers. The bedrooms or any extra side rooms are treated as the champagne rooms. Bouncers and other security are at the party as well, making sure things are done properly. Once time is up, the girls must get ready to go. A nice enough party can make you $1000 and better. I know of girls who made $3000 and more, just for two hours of work.

Quick Advice: Dancers don't have to help clean up or anything, that's the customer's problem.

BALLING ON A BUDGET

If you've been in this game long enough, or started off with little to no debts or financial obligations, you're going to want a few things for yourself. Many girls have never seen certain amounts of money at one time, especially if she's at an upscale spot, clocking $3000 or better a week. It's almost second nature for a person to get things they always wanted, just be smart about your splurging.

If you don't have this already, or want to upgrade into something better, one of those first wants is a car. When getting a car, I say it makes no sense to be flashy since you're a dancer. Be wise by getting either: a hybrid, a car with a four cylinder engine, or a car with a six cylinder engine that's great on gas, and easy to maintain. Low key cars like Honda Accords, Toyota Corollas, Chevy Impalas, or Ford Focuses are some examples.

With cars, you must not only save up for the vehicle itself, but also the insurance, dealership fees, title transfer, vehicle tag and registration. Decide whether you want to buy the car in full, or make payments through financing in order to build credit. Also, if you get a car from an auction, you must figure the cost to fix it.

Quick Advice: After you've made your first $1000, open a CD account for when saving for a car.

Another thing you'll want or need based on your situation, is your own place. You can choose to get either: an efficiency, apartment, condominium (condo), townhouse or house.

Efficiencies or apartments are cool to start off with when you first move out as a young person. With these options you pay rent, and depending on the location, you may pay for the electric and/or water bill as well.

Condos and town houses, especially in gated communities are a step up from an apartment. You'll pay more, but you get better security and amenities. Instead of rent, you'll pay a mortgage, an association fee, plus water and electric bills. You also must pay property taxes, but not as much as you would for a house.

Houses are things I urge you get after leaving the dancer game because it's a huge step. Most people get houses when they want to start a family, or begin real estate investing. With a house, along with bills, you pay a mortgage, property taxes, home owners insurance, plus maintenance of your home.

Quick Advice: Before getting your own place, take a course or read a book about real estate, and talk with a real estate lawyer. Get as many answers as possible before buying anything.

Urge To Splurge:

I know this is the "balling on a budget" section, but I strongly suggest you do this to get it out of your system. If you are on top of your bills, or have little to no responsibilities, buy a big ticket item you always wanted. Purchase something, or a bunch of things totaling $1000 - $5000. Be it a two week dream vacation, jewelry, a purse, or a bunch of clothes and shoes -- do it and think nothing of it.

Splurge just once, and that's it! Remember: the goal is to be out of this field in five years or less, so don't make big ticket spending a habit. Many girls try keeping up with the Joneses and never leave the club scene, so don't get caught up in what another girl bought. Plus, you never know when a drought will come, so splurging once, when the time is right is good enough.

Quick Advice: It's not how much your outfit costs, but how well you style it ladies. When buying clothes, resist all the high priced stuff, and shop at low cost stores. If you must shop at known department stores for name brand items, go to the clearance racks. In fact, you can call your favorite department stores, and ask the sales clerks or managers when clearance weeks are. Stores must mark down unsold items after a few weeks to make room for newer inventory.

It's going to be tough resisting your wants, so pay attention to the girls and people who have a plan -- keeping things low key. Have tunnel vision because temptations are out there. If you love yourself, keep to your monthly expenses, and what's left, save for the future. Dancers who are spendthrifts may advise you down the road to ruin, so keep your business to yourself.

Always focus on getting better at attracting, retaining and expanding on your clientele, and you'll never go broke in this business. The more you earn – the more you can save for that next major step.

CHAPTER 6:
MAPPING OUT AND
THEN ESCAPING

After two, three or even four years, you're a regular. You've traveled, partied a bit, saved a lot and learned from many strangers along the way. But now it's time to move on because your life is priceless, and your soul is precious regardless of what others think. It's time for you to step into a better future -- It's time for you to escape.

For those of you who never held down a real job, or worked for a short while before you started dancing, please take notes. This section is where you aim high in your goals and not shoot for any entry level gig, unless it's a stepping stone towards greater.

If you don't have any idea in what you want to do already, after your first year of dancing, try this exercise called "Soul Searching."

How to Soul Search:

First: Write down a list of all the careers or businesses that interest you most. It can be 5 or 105, just write them all down.

Second: With each one listed, research and critically think about what you want. Approach folks in those fields and ask a ton of questions.

Third: This sounds cliché, but do go after careers or business fields where you have a passion. Be it making quilts or growing flowers, if it's something you love, then it'll never feel like work. With passions you only want to get better. The more masterful you become in your craft, the more money you stand to make.

Quick Advice: As you're dancing, take the time reading books that are meaningful. The wealthiest people in the world read a lot. Self-help books, things they may invest in, or just for entertainment -- the wealthy top one percent we hear about in the media, read like crazy. Reading one or two powerful works can motivate or keep you motivated.

Here's a list of books I strongly suggest while Soul Searching:

- ➤ *A Purse of Your Own: An Easy Guide to Financial Security* by Deborah Owens
- ➤ *Mastery* by Robert Greene
- ➤ *The 50th Law* by 50 Cent & Robert Green
- ➤ *Think Big and Grow Rich* by Napoleon Hill
- ➤ *How to Win Friends and Influence People* by Dale Carnegie
- ➤ *The Art of War* by Sun Tzu
- ➤ *Who Moved My Cheese* by Spencer Johnson

- *The Alchemist* by Paulo Coelho
- *The History of Money* by Jack Weatherford
- *Steve Jobs* by Walter Isaacson
- *Freeway Ricky Ross: The Untold Autobiography* by Rick Ross
- *What I Learned Losing a Million Dollars* by Jim Paul, Brendan Moynihan, & Jack Schwager

NOTHING LIKE FAMILY

Even though this doesn't have anything to do with making money, if you're in good standing with family, take the time to invest quality time. Having a support network is great especially for your exit out. So while making it as a dancer, patch things up with those who care most because they only want to see you do right.

Never make the club your life. Some girls make people on the scene their makeshift family, especially those from dysfunctional homes and environments. There are girls who show up where they dance, on their nights off, to have fun with co-workers who're on shift.

Find a hobby, make yourself available for holidays, hang out with younger cousins, and remain close with friends who always had your back. Do whatever you can to keep a healthy balance, or semblance of a family unit.

Some girls know all too well the importance of family. There are dancers taking care of their families because their father and/or mother got sick, and the siblings are too young to work. But on the flipside, there are girls who aren't in good standing with family, bouncing from house to house, sleeping on couches and floors. They show up to the club on time, looking sexy, but are technically homeless until they get it together.

However your relationship with your family, please work to make things right. Some family members are extremely let down by your choice because they expected more from you. They love you, but time will decide the healing process. I'm sure as you're making your way out, finishing school or starting a business, your parent or loved one who kicked you out, will be your biggest supporter.

Quick Advice: Ladies who are in a relationship with a guy, you dance to support your brighter future to come, and not him. If the guy you're with is a jobless loser, leeching off you, get rid of him. If you have kids or sickly/older family, take care of them and not a grown man. A man must bring something to the table, or be a leader making moves or working someplace stable.

BACKGROUND CHECK

Before coming out, make sure your mind, body and criminal record is in order. If you have problems with alcohol, drugs, gambling or anything that can hurt you and/or others, please get help. Find a support group, get a psychiatrist and be honest.

Dancers with a juvenile record or one misdemeanor, depending on the charge, you can get that expunged or sealed. The process is different from state to state, so do some research. But if you have major violations on your adult record, you'll have trouble getting a job or entering school. I'm not saying you won't find a job, or get into a school by you having a criminal record, but the difficulty level does go up.

This is why I beg of you, never solicit yourself for money. It can break you down not only physically, but mentally for you know many have been with you in such an intimate fashion. Some women are mentally tough, while others end up in sad situations. Having a record for solicitation doesn't bode well, for you never know if the ones hiring are pious, or creeps trying to sleep with you later on down the line.

In case you didn't graduate high school, get your G.E.D (General Education Development) first. It'll be a great morale and self-esteem booster, plus with just about every career field, you'll need a diploma or G.E.D. Do not procrastinate, signup now and pass that test. Beauty and brains are a wonderful combination.

Any last bit of financial debt, get rid of it. If you have a car, pay off the note or buy the car out right from the beginning. Those with credit problems, get them in check because some places won't hire you with bad credit. All medical bills, dental bills, anything that you owe, pay it all off for your peace of mind.

Quick Advice: If you're a spiritual person or religion is major to you, give something back to God. No matter what religion you practice, just give back and give thanks.

SOME JUST-IN-CASE PAYBACK

Shady clubs try charging dancers unlawful fees, cheating them out of money needed during slow times, or a dancer's responsibilities. Certain fees charged by a club, if they don't sound right to you, research or check with a lawyer what the labor laws are. Check out www.licensepimp.com or look up the Fair Labor Standards Act at www.dol.gov to get some insight.

There are cases of dancers winning lawsuits, suing the clubs they worked for. If the paperwork you signed in the beginning states that you're an Independent Contactor (meaning you're self-employed), and the club is treating dancers like employees then you may have a case. Get in touch with a lawyer, gather up some girls who know they've been cheated, and see what happens.

If you signed on as an employee, by law an establishment must grant you at least two 10 – 15 minute breaks, and at least one

30 minute lunch break. Yes you remove your clothing for money, but you're still covered by the law. And never hesitate to call the Occupational Safety and Health Administration (OSHA), if the job environment isn't safe and up to code as well.

Quick Advice: All clubs that violated girls financially can be taken to court. But depending upon when the unlawful misdeeds occurred, and your state's statute of limitations, you may not have a case. Talk to a lawyer who specializes in labor laws and see what can be done.

CAREERS

There's a difference between a job and a career. Being an exotic dancer is a job, not a career, meaning its something temporary. A career is something you do for the rest of your life, make a decent wage and even support a family. In most careers you must posses or learn a skill, or a trade, in order for you to get ahead. But do know that there are levels to careers.

Certifications & Degrees

It will take you anywhere between two weeks on up to ten years, depending on what you're completing. There are people who I know that took 12 years or more, going part-time getting their degrees. But they stuck it through, and are happy they did because they're now in fields they truly want to be in.

Examples where a certification or two year degree is needed:

- Daycare workers
- Certified Nursing Assistants
- Medical Assistants
- Billing & Coding Specialist
- Dental Assistants
- Paralegals
- Pharmacy Technicians
- Cosmetologist
- Real Estate Agents
- Tax Preparers
- Bartenders
- Even security guards fall under this level.

Some options pay more than others, with few allowing you to start a small business from it. But with all of these aforementioned paths, you must first obtain a license, by first taking a state required test after passing a course from an accredited program.

The universe is the limit in terms of what you can do. I know dancers who became nurses. Others I know got their bachelor's degrees in criminal justice, business administration, or teaching. Some people got into corrections, the police academy, or became emergency medical techs. You can be what you set your mind to being, so don't be afraid to fill that role.

Quick Advice: Think outside the box if you aren't too happy about what I suggested in this section. You can be a chef, a funeral director, a journalist, a chiropractor or a lawyer. Just keep

searching until you find something that feels good to you. Find something that you'd stay up all night, and get up extra early the next day for because you want to make it work.

Business Entrepreneurs

The world is bigger than the club scene, so visualize being in another line of work. Once you're out, stick to your hustle regardless of how bad it may seem initially. In business, from what every successful entrepreneur has taught me is once you spot a need, you fill it. A great idea can come from anywhere, but seeing it through takes brains, heart, and the willingness to persevere. Negative voices will try talking you off your game.

But what's more important: you living life on your terms or you years later questioning what could've been?

I've seen former dancers succeed in these businesses:

- Hair and/or nail beauticians
- Real estate and mortgage brokerage firms
- Party planning & decorating
- Wig making
- Costume creating and seamstress work
- Pole dancing instructors
- Cleaning services for office buildings and those who can afford it
- Some sell dancing shoes with accessories to dancers

- I know one girl who got into financial advising plus trading stocks and bonds.

Quick Advice: The easier business field to transition into is hair and nails. Ladies are always looking for a good hair dresser and nail technician at great rates. If you can setup a shop big enough to not only do women's hair and nails, but also have a part for barbers giving guys haircuts, then you're almost guaranteed a chance at success. Plus, besides the time difference (unless you worked mostly day shift at a club), this field has the same busy days as the strip club, which are Fridays, Saturdays and Sundays.

You never know what field of business a person will get into. Believe it or not, some girls who were club bullies, with the worst attitudes, went on to become pastors of a church. But no matter the endeavor, know what kind you're getting into in terms of its structure. Find out the differences between a corporation, a limited liability corporation (LLC), sole proprietorship, and other business structures.

Draw up a business plan, and have agreements ready in case you're partnering up with someone. If you plan on having employees, formulate a chain of command with duties assigned to each job position in your company. Thoroughly plan this out, and if you slip on the little things, fix them fast.

Quick Advice: While planning and researching for your business, some books give you great insight from people who are winning.

Get the physical copy or audio book version of these titles:

- *Midas Touch: Why Some Entrepreneurs Get Rich and Why Most Don't* by Donald Trump & Robert Kiyosaki
- *Warren Buffet's Management Secrets: Proven Tools for Personal & Business Success* by Mary Buffett & David Clark
- *The Goal: A Process of Ongoing Improvement* by Eliyahu M. Goldratt and Jeff Cox

LAST CALL AND FAREWELL

Job Search

When seeking a job in your career of choice, have your resume and cover letters at ready. Your cover letter and the main portion of your resume must be no more than one page long. Your resume can have a second page, but that's only for recommendations upon request. Do not lie on your application or resume, for it may come back to hurt you.

A first impression lasts a lot longer than a second chance realization. If you can, take an interview etiquette course before job seeking, or follow these suggestions:

1. Get some rest the night before, for you want to be alert and sharp.
2. If you can, get a good 20 minute jog or 30 minute power walk to wake you up.
3. If you have kids, make sure they're with a babysitter or a person you can trust. Set everything up days before your interview.

4. If you can't make it, see about rescheduling the interview, but let them know at least 24 – 48 hours in advance.
5. Wear a business casual or business formal outfit, depending upon the job. Make sure your clothes are clean, ironed, and pressed. If you can, avoid wearing bright colors, or clothes that catches too much attention.
6. Keep you nails simple, and trim them down.
7. Unless you have vision problems, do not wear eye contacts, especially the colorful kind.
8. Don't wear high heels above three inches. If you want to play it safe, wear flats.
9. Don't wear sneakers to an interview regardless of the job field.
10. Shower and smell fresh, but don't wear heavy perfume or makeup.
11. Put your hair in a simple hairstyle like a ponytail or bun.
12. Don't show cleavage, or too much leg or thigh. If you're wearing a business dress skirt, make sure it isn't tight, and no shorter than a few inches above the knee.
13. If you're wearing slacks, make sure they aren't too tight. Covering up and being confident is the key.
14. Show up 15 – 20 minutes early, if not on time. You never know if parking or traffic will be hectic.
15. Cut your cell phone off! This shows unprofessionalism and lack of respect for the job if your cell rings during an interview.
16. Do not chew gum. If possible, floss then brush your teeth after having breakfast or lunch, keeping your breath as fresh as possible. If you do chew gum, spit it out before going into the interview room.

17. Shake the interviewers hand when you first walk-in, and always keep eye contact when speaking.
18. Answer all questions to the best of your ability. And be sure to emphasize how much you enjoy working with a team, and how much of a team player you are.
19. If you smoke cigarettes, avoid doing so until after the interview. You never know if the person dislikes cigarette smell.
20. Keep your knees together or legs crossed, and sit up straight when seated.
21. Try to keep a smile on your face, and have a positive disposition.
22. When speaking do not use slang terms. Be articulate, enunciate your words and avoid saying things like "um", "oh", or "know what I'm saying."
23. Unless they say otherwise, address the interviewer as sir or ma'am, Miss/Missus or Mister.
24. Don't rush your answers. Take your time when explaining or making a point.
25. Try not to flirt with the interviewer. You never want to come off as the office or job site slut.

Quick Advice: If you use marijuana, stop doing so 30 – 45 days before your interview so it can clear from your system. If you use hard drugs, get help because you don't want to be a functioning addict.

In certain scenarios, you may not land your dream job right away. Sometimes you have to get your foot in the door, doing a lower level gig then work your way up. Bide your time until what you want opens up. Once you're in, network with people, letting them know who you are for when the time comes, the right folks in power positions can vouch for you.

There are millionaires who started off in the mailrooms of Fortune 500 companies. There are entertainers who were the janitors of recording studios that made their way onto the top of the charts and box offices. Some people who started their own companies started off as interns. Get in where you can fit in, and then jump on your opportunity when it's right. Patients can go a long way, if you know how to utilize your time.

Building Business

Capitalizing on a passion is what makes entrepreneurs special. But before you incorporate what moves you, if you can, take a class or read a book on how to start a small business. Take classes or read about marketing your business, its products and/or services. Take classes on being a better sales person. Read about tax codes, understanding how tax cuts are given to thriving businesses. Get all the information you can because knowledge when applied properly leads to prosperity.

If you're a visual learner, there are tons of videos on YouTube that explain just about all aspects of business. You can use these as crash courses. So find a computer with an internet connection, have a pen and pad available and soak in as much information as possible. All of this learning will take you a few months to a few years, so don't wait just take that step by enrolling, clicking your mouse, or getting that book.

The money you make from dancing is considered "sweat equity." The main thing you'll be saving for in terms of business investment is Capital. Capital is the cash and/or assets (the wealth of a company), put into a business for generating income. With good credit, enough saved sweat equity, and/or if you have a home or two you can use as collateral, you may be able to get a Small Business Loan as well. Check with a financial advisor, and plan this part out carefully.

Not having enough equity or Capital can hold you back. It may delay your advancement, so if you're concentrated on leaving the club, stack your money. The more you have, along with a well thought out plan, the better your chances at succeeding. There are many people who saved money for several years, or had to get loans from family members and prayed to land a lucky break. I'm not saying being an exotic dancer is a great thing, but you have a much higher chance at quickly saving $100,000 toward a business than the average person, so be smart about it.

After finding then mastering your passion, and planning your business. After filing the right paper works, and understanding how much you'll need to promote and produce your business. And figuring out whether or not to rent an office space, or warehouse space you must get on your grind.

In the early stages, you may have to pull double duty. Meaning right after dancing most of the night, you'll have to get up later that morning to work your business. But when done correctly, customers will support you. In time, as money starts coming in, you'll slowly but surely make your way out the club.

Example:

Let's say you work five days a week at the club. Reduce it to four days at the club when your business can pay 20% of your personal monthly bills on a consist bases. For every additional 20% of personal monthly bill payment, after business expenses are paid first, you take off another day from working at the club.

In other words if your monthly personal bills total $1000, and your business can pay $200 per month every month, then take a day away from working the club. At $400 per month you take off two days, $600 per month you take away three days, and so on until you're out the club.

Many girls who start pulling out of the club life, often stop working at the clubs during the week to focus on their schooling, career or business. They usually work the clubs Friday – Sunday, or from Thursday - Saturday. As things get sweeter, they keep shortening their days at the club until they're never there again.

Remember some of the contacts you made while dancing for corporate customers and ballers. Depending on whom, these customers can either mentor you by giving sound business advice, or if you're business sounds viable, partner up with you. Guidance from someone who understands business can be your best asset.

In this game I've come across lawyers who specialized in business law, and accountants who worked with people who are self-employed. I've met stock brokers, project managers, and financial advisors. The point is you will come across people that may work with your company, so keep those business cards and contacts.

You never know who can be a con artist in a suit. Before seeking advice from these specialists check their credentials. Do some detective work, and find out how reputable they are by checking the Better Business Bureau. If you can, try to find out who these specialists have represented, and are they satisfied customers.

Quick Advice: When it comes to investing in a potential business venture, do not go all in so quickly. If you have $50,000 saved, unless you stumble across the next Microsoft or Vitamin Water, see what happens with a few hundred dollars and then add more into the investment after you've seen a return in the form of sales, or potential sales from those willing to pay right away. The main goal is to research and double if not triple check what you're getting into. There are clever people who come up with million

dollar Ponzi schemes every decade. So beware of what sounds too good to be true.

More Quick Advice: If you're looking into stocks and bonds, the main thing I can suggest is make sure you know the intentions of your stock broker. Brokers who aren't paid an hourly wage who keep trying to sell you certain stocks, over and over again are getting paid commission. Every time they sell a particular stock share, they get a check. Those paid on commission may not take the time finding the right stocks for your portfolio.

THAT FLIMFLAM SCAMS BUSINESS

The co-author of this manual is starting his business. He told me about a couple of scams or wannabe con artists trying to run game on him. Each person came with different angles, but had the same claim of them knowing millionaires or them helping others make millions of dollars.

One approached him on Facebook from a socially conscious angle, saying she knew millionaires who could invest in his business. He looked at her profile, and asked for credentials and names. The woman suggested he come to Atlanta (my co-writer and I are in Miami), and then they could talk business. He didn't answer back, and blocked her immediately.

The second flimflam scam person saw that he offers a finders fee to those who bring him ghostwriting, or book editing services above a certain dollar amount paid. The person asked for 20% of total sales from goods (books) and services (writing), if she helped promote his business online. My co-writer informed her that the fee is a one-time offer, and declined her proposition until she presented a success filled track record. The woman sounded off saying she has made millions for people, and that he will miss out on his chance. He kindly declined, and never saw that woman ever again.

In today's age and time, the biggest people in business conduct it however they can. Be it on the phone, face-to-face meeting, Skype, email, text, social media platform -- however, they will get in contact when there is a deal on the table worth their time. Plus in terms of credentials, successful business people pride themselves on being efficient, letting you know what moves they've made in becoming successful. As my co-writer said, "if they can't give you a clear-cut resume or have a consistent contact of some kind, then don't talk to them."

In time, you're going to begin hiring employees. You can have a one person private practice depending upon your specialty, but with most businesses, you're going to need a team. Hire people for their personality and not always on skill. If they appear to have commonsense, seem joyful and bubbly, then you can work with them. Never hire people who are skilled and are overly confident. These tend to be the ambitious types who feel they can run your whole company without you, but lack tact and grace.

You and another dancer may have similar business goals. Just make sure it's a passion of theirs as well. People who aren't serious about a goal are only well-wishing on a get-rich-quick scheme. There were plenty of businesses that ended before they even started because of this. A thriving business can take months or even years of hard work before any major return, so be patient. Hopefully you choose a field that can ensure a fast turn over.

Quick Advice: If you don't mind braving the elements, another way to make money in business is to sell items on the side of the road. Believe it or not, people who have hot dog carts, lunch trucks, or who sell bottles of water and other items, in the right location, make a decent amount of money each year. In Miami-Dade in order to sell items you need what is called a "peddlers license." Find out what licenses, forms, tax information, and registrations in your city you must fill out in order to be a street vendor.

Do not cut corners on the quality of your work. If word gets out that you sell bad product or improper service, you will not scale up your business. Think about it: Would people pay thousands of dollars for a Rolls-Royce if they knew the engine overheated every two weeks? No, I don't think so.

So keep your prices fair, and your work of great quality regardless of whose paying. In time, if you're of great quality, you can raise your rates little by little, or offer special prices for extra services.

Retirement & Peace of Mind

With whatever money you have left in your savings while exiting the club, look into retirement options. Research IRAs (Individual Retirement Accounts) or Roth IRAs, and 401k plans if you can. Get an understanding on how you can take care of yourself during your golden years.

With any path you take, be sure to never include negative people, or those who don't believe in themselves or their own causes. Those putting out negative energy and hopeless people are anchors who'll keep you stuck in one spot. They are big cancers you don't need. They'll weigh you down with complaints, and half-assed excuses, having you wonder if they've seen a happy moment in life.

Show love and be humble as you make your way toward certain success, but don't keep fake friends around you. You don't need a bandwagon -- you need those who'll keep you in the realm of reality. You want folks who are there for you genuinely, and not someone coming around once you make your way out.

I want to wrap this up with a hypothetical not real, metaphorical, short anecdote about two dancers. I pray it drives home the points I expressed in this manual. You don't have to take any advice given, but do know that a guide whose been where you want to be is better than no guide. Hope you appreciate what I'm doing for you because not many will be this honest.

Thanks for your interest in the naked hustle. And most importantly, thank you for seeking insight before making a move that may or may not be for you. I know I'm helping some of you ladies find your way toward prosperity, or maybe even redemption. Either way, once you get out, stay out because a well developed dependency on this game makes it harder for you to turn away. Let it go, and stay focused on your grind.

A Tale of Two Strippers

Red Hot, Love Jones and I entered the game around the same time, in the late 1990s early 2000s. I know I look good, but both these women were poetry in heels -- desired by most men they encountered. Both women kept the same long term customers for years at a time. Whenever a promoter wanted girls for out-of-town trips, they were always selected for the mansion and yacht parties.

Prior to 2007 - 2008, money was flowing, bills got paid and life was good. Red Hot used to drink with the best of them, and get high with the wildest of them. She would make $10,000, blow it all, then grind for what she lost and then some, all in a week. She feature danced at a lot of spots, and the DJs always wanted her to promote their events. I would say hi to her, and she'd say hello back; but unless you were with her crew, she wasn't overly friendly.

Love Jones was cool to be around. You can ask her for anything, and she'd be happy to help within her limits. She wasn't a pushover because she would curse you out if you overstepped boundaries. Other than a few times where Jones stood her ground, she was very professional about the job.

She made moves at more than one club and for a short while, feature danced for some of the international events. Love Jones only hung out with girls she respected. When she threw promotional parties, I never saw her get drunk or high.

After about two years in the business, Red Hot started dating guys who made their money in ways I wouldn't approve of. Love Jones kept things friendly with guys, but had eyes on a man she learned was in his third year in the military, who just started college. Red traveled everywhere, had guys spend tons of money on her, but she did things for that money that would make a porn star blush. Jones made moves at events that did great because of how she moved and operated.

By the time five years passed, Red started not looking the same. Facially she looked rough and started getting heavy, especially after having her third child. Love Jones started a daycare with the guy from the military who got his degree in social work. Besides a few minor stretch marks on her hip area, after her and her man's child was born, she still looks the same.

By the time 2011 came around, Red is now operating a lunch truck with her boyfriend who has kids as well. They serve food in front of the lower class spots she worked at before she gave up on dancing. Jones is married and the daycare her and current husband own, added a tutoring center for kids who need extra help.

They both got out the game. But Red is still in the rough parts of town, while Jones lives in the next county up, around 45 minutes away. Red's friends from her dancing days are still in those dive bars barely getting by, wondering what happened to all that money Red Hot made?

Jones had money to start a sizable nest egg and IRA, after the daycare really took off. She keeps things family oriented, and stays cordial with those she danced with. In fact, two of the girls she danced with work for her at the daycare, and they're both back in school.

Me, you may ask, "how am I living?" Well, I bounced from job to job after I left the club. I'm a grown woman going back to school for something I should've gotten years ago. But I'm not in the club anymore. I'm not where I want to be, but at least I'm doing what's needed to stay on track. I should get my certification soon. I'm studying for the state exams coming up. In a year's time, I should be doing better than I was yesterday.

I blew through more money than I should've, but at least I did enough to pay for my schooling now. Don't wait until it's too late for you. I pray to see you on top, and living a life worth experiencing. Good-bye to my naked hustle.

SPECIAL THANKS

I'd like to thank God for getting me through all these struggles, for without the struggle I wouldn't have stumbled across my strength. I'd like to thank my mother and sister, Marie E. Joseph and Romane Lynn. I'd like to thank my co-writer and business partner for his insights and skill sets.

I'd like to thank these dancers and club workers for their insights: Bay, Moe, Cherry, Serious, Nikki Jones, Baby Doll, Yoldie, Rampage, Coco, Cover Girl, Raven, Nya, Ginuwine, Tamika, Zoe, Zeus, Junior, DJ Jeff Fox, Kevin Miller, DJ Rok, DJ Juice, Billy Blue, Cutter Man, Chanel, Big Worm, Barbara (Worldwide Costume Extraordinaire), Shey, Nene, Lucretia, Hollywood, Caramel, Luscious, Sweet Heart, Brownin, DJ Shawty T, Pleasure, and Special (State to State, Special Exotic Costumes).

Another extra special thanks to my co-writer's mother and grandmother for allowing me time to reflect at their home, plus his brother for letting us use his laptop. Anyone else I forgot, I apologize but thank you for being there. And I would like to thank those who looked down on me, for you guys gave me all the inspiration I needed.

For business inquiries and speaking engagements contact here:

http://www.djehutiwritingandpublishing.com/

Nicholas Brown Contact

Company email: djehutiwritingandpublishing@gmail.com

Nicholas's Instagram: @djehutiwritingandpublishingllc

Office: 786-320-5936   Cell: 305-494-1349

Contact Elsa:

Cell: 786-371-6508

Direct email: lefemmelashay@gmail.com

https://instagram.com/lefemmelashay/

Twitter: @LefemmeLashay

LIKE on Facebook:

https://www.facebook.com/GirlNextDoorToPoleDancingDiva

Sandra Jean-Pierre:

http://tbwecovers.com/

tbwecovers@gmail.com

Made in the U.S.A.

Miami, FL

28 December 2015

Printed in Great Britain
by Amazon